Driven to Serve:

The Psychology of Motivation in Policing

By

Dr. Raimundo Socorro

"It is not the obligatory character of the rule laid down by an individual that makes us respect this individual. It is the respect we feel for the individual that makes us regard as obligatory the rule he lays down."

By Jean Piaget

Dedication

To my children — Brandon, Joseph, Alexandra, and Javier —

You are my world.

In the only way I know how, I have tried to show you that I love you — not just in words, but through action, sacrifice, and example. Every page of this book is a quiet echo of that effort, a testament to a life spent striving to make things better than how I found them.

You make me proud every day — not only for what you have achieved, but for who you have become.

May this work stand as a reflection of the values I've tried to instill in you: purpose, integrity, and the courage to lead with compassion. And may you always know that I am here for you — in this life and beyond.

With all my love,

Dad

About the Author

Dr. Raimundo Socorro is a distinguished law enforcement professional and educator with over three decades of experience in public safety, leadership, and academic excellence. His career seamlessly integrates commanding elite law enforcement units, such as S.W.A.T., and directing premier public safety education programs at major academic institutions.

As a former Commander of the Miami Police Department's S.W.A.T. and Hostage Negotiation Teams, Dr. Socorro oversaw high-stakes operations, including dignitary protection, tactical missions, and critical incident management. His strategic leadership reduced operational costs while enhancing team efficiency and public safety outcomes. Over his law enforcement career, Dr. Socorro held multiple leadership roles, commanding units such as Personnel Resource Management, Communications, and specialized task forces, consistently achieving operational excellence and community impact.

Equally notable are Dr. Socorro's contributions to academia and public service education. As the Dean of the School of Justice, Public Safety, and Law Studies at Miami Dade College, he managed one of the nation's leading public safety training centers. He directed academic and professional development programs, including degree tracks, certification courses, and an assessment center responsible for promotional and entry-level testing. Under his leadership, the center secured significant contracts with public service organizations, developing, administering, and ranking candidates for promotions, ensuring transparency and equity in these critical processes.

At Indian River State College, Dr. Socorro further advanced public safety education as Dean of Public Service Education and later as Director of International Training and Programs. Overseeing one of the most comprehensive public safety training complexes in the nation, he led efforts to provide advanced training for first responders and fostered international collaborations to elevate the standards of public safety worldwide.

Dr. Socorro's expertise extends globally, consulting and training agencies in tactical operations, leadership, and procedural justice. His passion for education and public service reflects a commitment to bridging the gap between law enforcement and the communities they serve. With a robust portfolio of achievements in law enforcement and education, Dr. Socorro exemplifies the fusion of field expertise and academic innovation, making him a valuable leader and advocate for public safety excellence.

Table of Contents

Dedication........ i

About the Author........ ii

Foreword........ 1

Introduction........ 3

Chapter 1: Theories of Motivation in Psychology........ 5

Chapter 2: The Achievement-Driven Officer: Understanding McClelland in Practice........ 21

Chapter 3: Detectives vs. Patrol Officers: Autonomy, Complexity, and Purpose........ 37

Chapter 4: Measuring What Matters: The Achievement Motivation Inventory (AMI) and Beyond........ 50

Chapter 5: Power, Affiliation, and the Dark Side of Motivation........ 73

Chapter 6: Motivation and the Ethical Compass........ 87

Chapter 7: Culture as the Crucible of Motivation........ 100

Chapter 8: Leading for Motivation: Organizational Strategies That Work........ 119

Chapter 9: Motivation in Crisis: Resilience, Burnout, and Purpose 139

Chapter 10: Training for Motivation—From Academy to Promotion........ 150

Chapter 11: Motivation Across Borders: International Policing Perspectives........ 166

Chapter 12: The Future of Motivation in Policing........ 179

References........ 198

Foreword

In a profession that demands courage, discipline, and unwavering integrity, few have approached the challenge of police leadership and officer development with the thoughtfulness and intellectual rigor of Dr. Raimundo Socorro. Over nearly three decades with the Miami Police Department, Ray distinguished himself not only as a skilled tactician and respected commander but as a transformative thinker committed to evolving the very culture of policing.

I had the privilege of working alongside Dr. Socorro during my tenure as Deputy Chief of Police in Miami. In every conversation and decision, Ray exhibited a rare blend of operational acumen and human insight. He understood what many fail to see: that the future of policing depends not only on tactics and technology, but on the hearts and minds of those who take the oath. In this way, Driven to Serve is both timely and deeply personal as a culmination of lived experience, academic scholarship, and an unwavering belief in the power of motivation to shape professional excellence.

Through this work, Dr. Socorro applies psychological theory to a world where lives, communities, and public trust are on the line. From McClelland's Three Needs Theory to real-world case studies of officer behavior, this book offers a groundbreaking framework for understanding what drives police officers, whether they are in patrol cars, detective bureaus, or command staff roles. He tackles critical questions about ethics, leadership, organizational culture, and mental health with clarity and purpose.

What truly sets this book apart is the spirit behind it. Ray has always believed in the calling of public service, not as a job, but as a vocation. He knows that the best officers are those who are driven by more than authority; they are driven by purpose, by community, and by an internal compass calibrated toward service.

At the heart of Ray's philosophy is a deep commitment to accountability, both departmental and personal, as non-negotiable pillars of legitimacy. True Procedural Justice does not exist in theory alone; it must be demonstrated in the day-to-day behavior of leaders and officers alike. Agencies that seek legitimacy in the eyes of the public must begin by cultivating internal cultures where transparency, ethical conduct, and self-assessment are not aspirations but expectations. This book speaks directly to that challenge, showing how motivation and accountability can coexist to build departments that earn trust and model integrity from within.

Driven to Serve is more than a contribution to police literature; it is a guide for the next generation of public safety professionals and the leaders who will shape them. For any agency serious about meaningful reform, sustainable morale, and building a culture of excellence, this book provides both the language and the roadmap.

I am proud to call Dr. Socorro a colleague, a thought partner, and above all, a leader who never stopped asking the deeper questions about who we are, why we serve, and how we grow.

Frank G. Fernandez
Deputy Chief of Police, Miami Police Department (Ret.)
Chief of Police, Hollywood Police Department (Frm.)
Director of Public Safety, Coral Gables Police and Fire Rescue (Frm.)

Introduction

In the high-stakes, emotionally charged world of policing, understanding what drives individuals to pursue and sustain a career in public safety is both a psychological inquiry and a practical imperative. Law enforcement officers operate under conditions that test physical endurance, emotional stability, and moral judgment. The decision to enter this field—and to remain committed in the face of danger, scrutiny, and increasing social complexity—is rarely a matter of salary or job convenience alone. Rather, it reflects deeper internal motivators, often rooted in personal values, social identity, and a sense of purpose.

Motivation—the inner drive that directs behavior—has been extensively studied in psychology, spanning early behaviorist approaches to contemporary cognitive, social, and humanistic theories. Classic theories, such as Maslow's hierarchy of needs or Herzberg's two-factor theory, provide a foundational lens to understand what individuals strive for and what conditions foster satisfaction or frustration. More nuanced frameworks, like David McClelland's Three Needs Theory, move beyond general needs to identify dominant motivational drivers—achievement, affiliation, and power—that shape how individuals engage with their roles.

When applied to the policing profession, these motivational theories do more than explain why someone becomes a cop; they illuminate how officers respond to challenges, interact with colleagues and communities, adapt to leadership roles, and navigate ethical dilemmas. In an era when police departments face unprecedented calls for reform, transparency, and community legitimacy, understanding the motivational landscape of those who serve becomes not just an academic exercise but a cornerstone of organizational effectiveness and public trust. These calls have been intensified by high-profile incidents such as the murder of George Floyd in 2020, which triggered global protests and prompted numerous Department of Justice consent decrees across the United States. Such events have highlighted the urgent need to understand and address the motivational and ethical dimensions of police behavior.

Chapter 1: Theories of Motivation in Psychology

Motivation theory has evolved considerably over the past century, offering increasingly sophisticated models to explain why people behave the way they do in organizational and social contexts. These theories are commonly categorized into three main types: content theories, process theories, and contemporary theories. Each group offers distinct insights into the motivational drivers behind human action—insights that are particularly valuable when applied to the unique demands of the policing profession.

Content Theories of Motivation

Content theories focus on identifying specific factors that motivate individuals. These theories seek to understand what needs or goals people are trying to satisfy. Among the most foundational content theories is Abraham Maslow's Hierarchy of Needs (1943), which posits that individuals are motivated by a progression of needs, from physiological and safety needs to love and belonging, esteem, and ultimately self-actualization. In the law enforcement context, Maslow's model helps explain how officers may initially be drawn by job stability and benefits, then stay committed due to deeper needs like belonging to a team, achieving respect, and fulfilling a sense of purpose through community service.

Another important content theory is Clayton Alderfer's ERG Theory, which refines Maslow's five levels into three core needs: Existence, Relatedness, and Growth. ERG theory allows for more flexibility than Maslow's rigid hierarchy, acknowledging that multiple needs may be pursued simultaneously—a dynamic particularly relevant in high-pressure fields like policing.

Frederick Herzberg's Two-Factor Theory (1966) further deepens our understanding by categorizing workplace factors into "hygiene" (extrinsic) factors—such as salary, working conditions, and job security—and "motivators" (intrinsic), like achievement, recognition, responsibility, and the nature of the work itself. Herzberg's theory is especially applicable to law enforcement, where poor hygiene factors can lead to dissatisfaction, but the absence of motivators can sap morale and purpose even in seemingly secure positions.

David McClelland's Theory of Needs (1961) is among the most relevant to policing. It identifies three dominant motivational needs: achievement (nAch), affiliation (nAff), and power (nPow). Unlike Maslow and Herzberg, McClelland emphasizes that these needs are acquired over time and can vary depending on one's experiences and role. Officers driven by achievement may excel in investigative or leadership roles, while those motivated by affiliation may thrive in community engagement, and those seeking power may gravitate toward supervisory or tactical positions. Socorro (2012) applied this framework in a study of urban police officers in Florida, finding distinct motivational profiles between patrol officers and detectives, with implications for role assignment and professional development.

Other content theories relevant to public safety include McGregor's Theory X and Theory Y, which outline contrasting assumptions about workers' motivations (authoritarian vs. participative styles), and Murray's Manifest Needs Theory, which laid early groundwork for later theories by emphasizing individualized, socially-learned needs.

Process Theories of Motivation

Process theories focus on the cognitive processes that influence decision-making and behavioral direction. Rather than asking what motivates people, these theories ask "how" motivation occurs.

One of the most influential is Victor Vroom's Expectancy Theory (1964), which posits that motivation depends on the belief that effort will lead to performance, that performance will lead to desired outcomes, and that those outcomes are valued. In policing, this theory helps explain why some officers are highly motivated in certain assignments but disengaged in others—especially when they perceive a lack of reward or recognition tied to their performance.

Equity Theory (Adams, 1963) suggests that people are motivated by fairness. Officers constantly compare their inputs (training, effort, risk) and outcomes (pay, promotions, respect) with those of others. Perceptions of inequity can breed resentment, disengagement, or misconduct—especially in environments where favoritism or unequal disciplinary practices are perceived.

For example, Vroom's Expectancy Theory can help explain the decline in motivation among officers working in chronically underfunded departments. When officers perceive that their efforts will not lead to recognition, advancement, or improved working conditions, their drive to perform above baseline expectations diminishes. Similarly, Equity Theory often manifests when junior officers observe senior colleagues receiving preferential treatment or disproportionate rewards, leading to a corrosive sense of unfairness that undermines cohesion and morale.

Goal-Setting Theory (Locke & Latham, 1990) posits that setting specific, challenging goals enhances performance, particularly when individuals are committed to them and receive regular feedback. Supervisors who engage officers in meaningful goal-setting—such as solving a backlog of cases, leading a public initiative, or completing a certification—can enhance motivation through a sense of accomplishment and mastery.

Reinforcement Theory (Skinner, 1953), though behaviorist in origin, still plays a role in policing through formal discipline and reward systems. Officers learn what behaviors are rewarded or punished, and they shape their conduct accordingly.

Contemporary Theories and Integrations

Contemporary motivation theories build upon and refine earlier models to address more dynamic and holistic understandings of human behavior.

Self-Determination Theory (Deci & Ryan, 1985) has gained prominence in public service contexts. It distinguishes between intrinsic motivation (driven by interest and enjoyment) and extrinsic motivation (driven by rewards and punishments). Crucially, it identifies three core psychological needs: autonomy, competence, and relatedness. Officers who feel empowered to make decisions, who feel capable and trained, and who feel connected to their team and community, are more likely to be intrinsically motivated—leading to greater job satisfaction and ethical behavior.

Job Characteristics Theory (Hackman & Oldham, 1976) emphasizes the design of the work itself. Five core dimensions—skill variety, task identity, task significance, autonomy, and feedback—contribute to meaningful work and high internal motivation. Applied to law enforcement, this theory suggests that rotating assignments, meaningful community interaction, and regular feedback can enhance intrinsic motivation.

Lastly, Public Service Motivation Theory (Perry & Wise, 1990) is especially salient in policing. It posits that individuals with high levels of public service motivation are driven by commitment to public values, compassion, self-sacrifice, and the desire to make a difference. Socorro's (2012) research supports this, showing that even among officers with differing dominant motivational profiles, many cited service and social impact as central to their identity and resilience.

Together, these theories create a multidimensional framework to understand what drives law enforcement professionals. In such a high-stress, high-visibility career, recognizing and supporting diverse motivational drivers is not merely about individual satisfaction—it is essential to fostering effective, ethical, and enduring public safety institutions.

McClelland's Three Needs Theory in Policing

David McClelland's theory suggests that individuals are motivated primarily by one of three needs:

- Need for Achievement (nAch): A drive to excel, achieve in relation to a set of standards, and strive to succeed. Officers with high nAch often seek out challenging tasks, set personal goals, and value performance feedback.

- Need for Affiliation (nAff): A desire for friendly and close interpersonal relationships. Such officers may gravitate toward community policing roles or units that emphasize teamwork and collaboration.

- Need for Power (nPow): The urge to influence or control others. This need can manifest as personal power (ego-driven) or institutional power (driven by a desire to organize efforts and achieve mission goals).

In the research study by Socorro (2012), "Achievement Motivation of Police Officers in a Florida Urban Setting," the application of McClelland's framework revealed significant differences in motivation between patrol officers and detectives. Using the Achievement Motivation Inventory (AMI), the study found that detectives scored significantly higher on scales measuring goal setting, independence, and internality—key indicators of high nAch orientation. Patrol officers, by contrast, scored higher on factors related to affiliation and responsiveness, reflecting a different motivational profile.

These findings support the notion that role specialization within law enforcement is partly shaped by underlying motivational drivers. Detectives, driven by a need for achievement, may be more intrinsically motivated by solving complex cases, while patrol officers may operate under a mix of affiliation (serving the community) and power (exercising authority in dynamic environments).

Motivation and Identity in Policing

Motivation does more than direct behavior—it profoundly shapes professional identity. In law enforcement, where roles are imbued with moral authority, legal responsibility, and community visibility, the question of *who an officer is* is deeply intertwined with *why they serve*. Officers often define themselves not simply by their title or duties, but by their perceived capacity to serve, protect, lead, and solve problems within the communities they are sworn to uphold.

This identity is not static; it is continuously reinforced or eroded through day-to-day experiences, leadership structures, peer dynamics, and public interactions. When an officer's internal motivation aligns with role expectations and the organizational culture, a sense of coherence, pride, and purpose often emerges. Officers who feel they are making a meaningful contribution—whether by preventing crime, mentoring youth, resolving domestic disputes, or investigating complex cases—report higher job satisfaction and a stronger sense of professional resilience. These officers are more likely to stay committed during periods of organizational stress or public criticism because their work aligns with their deeper values and purpose. In contrast, when motivation is stifled by bureaucratic inefficiencies, toxic leadership, or community mistrust, the officer's identity may begin to fragment—leading to disengagement, ethical compromise, or burnout. Thus, maintaining this alignment between motivation, identity, and institutional support is essential not just for individual well-being but for the health and legitimacy of the organization as a whole.

Conversely, when there is a misalignment between personal motivation and occupational reality, psychological and ethical strain can result. Officers driven by the need for affiliation may feel isolated in rigid, hierarchical environments. Those with a high need for achievement may become disillusioned when bureaucratic obstacles prevent goal attainment or innovation. Those seeking institutional power for the purpose of team improvement may become cynical if leadership opportunities are unavailable or unresponsive to their efforts. Over time, this misalignment can lead to a loss of purpose, diminished morale, and even adversarial attitudes toward the very institution they once sought to serve.

In some cases, it may manifest as passive compliance, reduced productivity, or active resistance to change. Left unaddressed, these motivational mismatches can erode organizational cohesion, increase turnover, and contribute to misconduct or apathy. Recognizing and addressing these disconnects is therefore critical for cultivating a healthy, motivated, and ethically grounded police workforce.

David McClelland's Theory of Needs offers a uniquely dynamic lens for interpreting this motivational-identity nexus. His model acknowledges that dominant motivational needs—achievement, affiliation, and power—are not only socially acquired but also subject to evolution throughout an individual's career trajectory (McClelland, 1961). This perspective is critical for policing, where the roles, risks, and rewards shift substantially over time.

For example, an officer early in their career might be motivated by a strong need for power (nPow), seeking to assert authority, restore order, or lead operations. As that officer gains experience, they may develop a heightened need for achievement (nAch), becoming more goal-oriented, focused on solving cases, acquiring credentials, or supervising units. In later stages, particularly as personal values mature and professional networks deepen, affiliation (nAff) may become more prominent, leading some to seek roles that emphasize mentorship, community engagement, or organizational stewardship. This progression reflects not only personal growth but also an evolving understanding of the profession's broader impact. Officers who once prioritized command and control may later find fulfillment in building relationships, fostering teamwork, and shaping the next generation of law enforcement. This dynamic shift underscores the importance of flexible leadership and career pathways that accommodate changing motivational drivers over time, ensuring that officers remain engaged, effective, and aligned with the mission of public service.

This motivational evolution plays a key role in how officers cope with stress, interpret challenges, and find meaning in their work. Officers who understand their own motivational drivers—and work in environments that support their developmental trajectory—are better equipped to adapt, lead ethically, and avoid burnout. Supervisors who recognize the motivational profiles of their team members can assign roles more strategically, foster better morale, and facilitate professional growth. For instance, an officer with a high need for achievement might thrive when given investigative responsibilities or opportunities to lead special projects, while an officer driven by affiliation may excel in community outreach or peer support roles. Similarly, those motivated by power can be guided toward leadership tracks that emphasize ethical influence and organizational improvement. When supervisory decisions align with these underlying motivational drivers, the result is a more resilient, engaged, and high-performing workforce. Ultimately, understanding and leveraging motivational diversity within a department is not only a tool for individual development—it is a strategic imperative for building effective and adaptive police organizations.

The concept of "role identity" is also central here. Role identity theory suggests that people internalize the expectations associated with their roles, shaping how they behave, how they see themselves, and how they believe others perceive them (Stryker & Burke, 2000).

In policing, this means that officers who are consistently treated as community guardians, valued professionals, or ethical leaders are more likely to internalize and act according to those expectations. The opposite is also true: if organizations reinforce negative stereotypes, emphasize aggressive enforcement over service, or treat officers as expendable enforcers rather than trusted public servants, those messages can become embedded in how officers perceive themselves and their roles. This internalized identity can influence decision-making, interpersonal interactions, and ethical standards—either positively or negatively. In the absence of supportive role modeling and affirming institutional culture, officers may adopt defensive or authoritarian postures, distancing themselves from the communities they serve and becoming more susceptible to cynicism or misconduct. Therefore, the cultivation of positive role identity must be an intentional process, embedded in training, leadership, and everyday organizational practices that affirm the value, integrity, and societal importance of the policing profession.

Motivation and identity, therefore, operate in a reciprocal relationship. Officers bring with them certain motivational tendencies, which shape their experiences and decisions. Those experiences, in turn, reinforce or reshape their self-concept. If this cycle is supported by ethical leadership, meaningful assignments, and recognition of individual differences, it can build not only strong individual identities but resilient organizational cultures.

Understanding this interplay is essential for anyone invested in police leadership, training, and reform. Fostering environments where officers can pursue achievement, experience meaningful affiliation, and exercise ethical power is not merely an issue of job satisfaction—it is a matter of institutional integrity and public trust.

The Public Service Calling

One of the most enduring and powerful motivational constructs in policing is the idea of a "public service calling." Unlike external motivators such as salary, benefits, or job stability, a calling represents an internalized sense of purpose that compels individuals to contribute to something greater than themselves. In policing, this often takes the form of a deep-rooted commitment to community safety, justice, and societal well-being. Officers driven by this calling frequently view their role as not just a job, but as a vocation—an expression of their values and a means of making a meaningful difference in the lives of others. This intrinsic motivation often shapes how they approach challenges, interact with the public, and navigate ethical dilemmas. Officers who perceive their work as a calling are more likely to demonstrate resilience under pressure, maintain high moral standards, and remain committed to the long-term well-being of the communities they serve. This sense of purpose not only sustains individual officers through the hardships of the profession but also contributes to the legitimacy and trustworthiness of law enforcement institutions as a whole.

The concept of public service motivation (PSM) was formally conceptualized by Perry and Wise (1990), who defined it as a specific form of prosocial motivation rooted in the values of public institutions. PSM is characterized by four key dimensions: attraction to public policy making, commitment to the public interest, compassion, and self-sacrifice. Individuals with high PSM are drawn to roles where they can help others, advance collective welfare, and uphold moral values—even at personal cost. In the context of policing, this means that officers with high levels of PSM may willingly take on challenging assignments, intervene in volatile situations, or go above and beyond their duties—not for recognition or reward, but because they believe deeply in the mission of justice and service. Their actions are guided by a moral compass that prioritizes the needs of the community, especially the vulnerable and marginalized. When law enforcement agencies actively cultivate and support this type of motivation—through ethical leadership, meaningful community engagement, and recognition of altruistic service—they not only reinforce individual commitment but also strengthen institutional legitimacy and public trust.

For many officers, this intrinsic motivation begins well before they enter the academy. It is often shaped by formative experiences—such as exposure to crime, injustice, or positive role models in law enforcement—or by a general sense of civic responsibility. Once in the profession, this sense of calling becomes a critical resource, especially in high-stress or morally ambiguous situations. Officers who perceive their work as meaningful are more likely to exhibit perseverance, ethical integrity, and empathy.

In environments where organizational leadership acknowledges and nurtures this motivation, the benefits are manifold. Officers report higher levels of job satisfaction, organizational commitment, and psychological resilience. Conversely, when leadership fails to recognize this intrinsic drive—or worse, undermines it through corruption, politicization, or excessive bureaucracy—officers may become disillusioned, detached, or ethically compromised. Thus, leadership and organizational culture play a pivotal role.

The idea of policing as a calling is also closely tied to the concept of "servant leadership," a philosophy that prioritizes the well-being of the community and the development of subordinates over personal or institutional power. Servant leaders in law enforcement not only reinforce the legitimacy of public service motivation but also create environments where officers feel empowered to act in alignment with their values.

Socorro's (2012) study on achievement motivation among police officers in a Florida urban setting offers important empirical support for this perspective. While the study revealed variance in dominant motivational needs—achievement, affiliation, and power—many participants, regardless of their individual profiles, articulated a sense of duty to serve and protect as central to their identity. Officers frequently cited their impact on the community, their ability to de-escalate conflict, and their role in resolving problems as sources of personal fulfillment and professional pride. These accounts suggest that, beyond their individual motivational drivers, officers are often unified by a shared belief in the value and meaning of their work. This intrinsic connection to service acts as a stabilizing force, helping officers navigate stress, adversity, and organizational challenges. Socorro's findings underscore the importance of recognizing and nurturing this internalized sense of purpose—not only during recruitment and academy training, but throughout the officer's career—through mentorship, ethical leadership, and organizational practices that reinforce the nobility of service.

Moreover, the resilience observed among these officers—despite stress, limited resources, and organizational challenges—was often tied to their belief in the social importance of their role. This underscores the importance of reinforcing public service calling not just during recruitment, but throughout the career lifecycle, through policies, mentorship, training, and recognition programs that elevate ethical and community-centered work.

In a time when public scrutiny of law enforcement is high and morale in many departments is under strain, reaffirming the legitimacy and value of the public service calling can be a stabilizing force. It serves as both a moral compass and a motivational engine, guiding officers through challenges while anchoring them to a deeper professional and civic identity. When aligned with strong leadership and ethical institutional frameworks, the public service calling not only sustains the individual but also fortifies the profession itself—promoting resilience, ethical conduct, and a long-term commitment to community trust. Departments that nurture this intrinsic sense of purpose are more likely to foster cultures of integrity, attract purpose-driven recruits, and weather the sociopolitical challenges that so often test the legitimacy of policing. In this way, the public service calling becomes not just a personal motivator, but a structural pillar that supports healthy law enforcement organizations and a more just society.

Conclusion

Understanding what drives a cop goes far beyond the simplistic lens of job satisfaction surveys or retention statistics. While such instruments may capture surface-level attitudes, they often fail to uncover the deeper psychological mechanisms that sustain or erode a law enforcement officer's sense of purpose, performance, and ethical commitment. Motivation in policing must be understood as a layered, evolving, and highly contextual phenomenon—rooted not only in individual personality and experiences but also in the institutional, cultural, and community dynamics that shape the profession.

As explored throughout this chapter, motivational theories in psychology—from foundational content models to sophisticated contemporary frameworks—offer essential tools for decoding the internal drivers of law enforcement professionals. These theories help distinguish between surface-level compliance and deep, enduring commitment. They also clarify why some officers thrive under pressure, demonstrate compassion in high-stakes environments, and uphold public trust, while others struggle with disengagement, cynicism, or even ethical collapse.

Among these theoretical models, David McClelland's Three Needs Theory stands out for its unique applicability to law enforcement. By focusing on the learned and dominant needs for achievement, affiliation, and power, McClelland provides a flexible framework that acknowledges the complex and shifting motivations that shape police work. His theory allows us to understand why detectives may be driven by problem-solving and goal attainment, why patrol officers may find meaning in community interaction and visible presence, and why leaders may be fueled by the structured use of institutional authority to support their teams and safeguard the public.

Moreover, this framework reminds us that motivation is not static. Officers enter the profession with certain motivations, but these can and often do change based on personal development, organizational support, exposure to trauma, and career stage. An officer initially driven by power and control may, over time, evolve toward seeking affiliation or mastery. Recognizing this evolution is essential for leadership, training, and wellness initiatives that aim to align personal development with professional role expectations and institutional mission.

When such motivation is aligned with a genuine public service ethos—the belief in service beyond self, in justice beyond enforcement—it transforms from an internal engine into a moral and operational compass. It guides officers in decision-making, anchors them during ethical dilemmas, and fuels resilience in the face of danger, scrutiny, and stress. Officers motivated by this public service calling are more likely to act with integrity, maintain long-term engagement, and contribute to the legitimacy and ethical standing of their departments.

Importantly, law enforcement agencies that recognize, support, and strategically develop motivational strengths within their ranks are better equipped to build trust with the public, cultivate ethical leadership, and create resilient organizational cultures. Motivation, then, is not merely a topic for psychological theory—it is a strategic imperative for modern policing. It is a foundational lens through which we can better understand officer behavior, reform institutional practices, and ultimately reimagine what it means to protect and serve in the 21st century.

Chapter 2: The Achievement-Driven Officer: Understanding McClelland in Practice

Introduction

In a field as complex and high-stakes as law enforcement, understanding what drives individual officers can be the key to unlocking not only their potential but also the effectiveness of the department as a whole. Law enforcement personnel operate in environments characterized by unpredictability, danger, and public scrutiny. These conditions demand more than just physical readiness—they require deep psychological resilience, ethical consistency, and motivational endurance. Officers are not a monolithic group; they bring to the profession varied personal goals, emotional responses, and cognitive frameworks that shape how they perceive their duties and how they perform them.

One of the most influential psychological models for unpacking these individual differences is David McClelland's Achievement Motivation Theory. This theory, part of a broader framework on human motivation, categorizes individuals based on three primary needs: achievement, affiliation, and power. Among these, the need for achievement (nAch) stands out as particularly relevant for understanding exceptional performance in policing. Officers with a high need for achievement are motivated not by external rewards or fear of failure, but by a desire to meet personal standards of excellence. They prefer situations where outcomes are contingent on their own efforts, thrive when given challenging but attainable goals, and seek feedback to continually improve.

Particularly, the need for achievement (nAch) offers insight into how and why certain officers excel under pressure, pursue specialized roles, and respond uniquely to stress and organizational demands. These officers are not content with routine or mediocrity; instead, they actively seek roles that allow them to stretch their capabilities, solve complex problems, and make a measurable impact. Whether it's the detective meticulously building a case, the field training officer mentoring new recruits, or the SWAT team member perfecting tactical precision, high nAch officers are often the backbone of progressive law enforcement agencies. Their motivation fuels innovation, persistence, and ethical conduct, especially in situations where split-second decisions can have life-altering consequences. Understanding this motivational drive is critical not only for officer development but also for leadership, recruitment, and retention strategies that align departmental goals with individual purpose.

Organizations that recognize and cultivate achievement motivation among their personnel can build a more competent, resilient, and adaptive workforce. This means not only identifying high-achieving officers but also creating an environment in which they can thrive—through goal-oriented feedback, opportunities for advancement, and assignments that provide autonomy and challenge. Conversely, ignoring the motivational needs of officers may lead to disengagement, stagnation, or attrition, particularly among those with the highest potential for growth. In the current climate of law enforcement reform, where transparency, effectiveness, and community trust are under the microscope, leveraging internal motivation becomes a strategic imperative. When departments invest in understanding what drives their officers, they unlock pathways to professional excellence, organizational integrity, and public confidence.

The Psychology of the High-Achiever in Uniform

David McClelland argued that individuals with a high need for achievement are internally motivated to pursue excellence, prefer tasks with moderate difficulty, and seek out environments where outcomes are clearly linked to their own efforts (McClelland, 1961). In law enforcement, these traits translate into a unique professional mindset. High-achieving officers are often the ones who go beyond the bare minimum, volunteering for additional responsibilities, seeking out specialized training, and striving to be evaluated on their personal merits.

They tend to measure success in terms of progress and mastery rather than rank or external accolades. Their internal scorecard often focuses on problem-solving efficiency, accuracy of decisions under pressure, and their ability to contribute meaningfully to the department's mission. These officers often exhibit a forward-leaning posture toward professional development, including pursuing certifications, advanced degrees, or lateral skills that enhance their competence. Their behavior is often characterized by initiative, persistence, and a strong sense of ownership over the outcomes of their work.

Patrol officers and detectives often manifest achievement differently. Patrol officers with high achievement motivation may set performance goals such as rapid response times, accurate reporting, and proactive problem-solving in the field. They may routinely de-escalate volatile situations with precision or take extra initiative during community policing efforts. Detectives, on the other hand, may thrive on solving complex cases, seeking resolution in investigations that require perseverance, insight, and cognitive challenge. They often demonstrate a tenacious attention to detail, a passion for uncovering the truth, and an appreciation for work that requires sustained effort over long periods.

Consider the case of Officer Ramirez, who consistently closes narcotics investigations through patient surveillance and community engagement. While her peers rotate through different assignments, she insists on staying with long-term investigations. Her intrinsic drive is not about recognition, but rather about achieving personal mastery in her field—a hallmark of the achievement-motivated personality. Ramirez's daily routines—logging patterns, cultivating informants, refining warrant language—reflect an internal compass oriented toward excellence. Her colleagues describe her as "obsessed with the case," not because of ego, but because of a deeply personal commitment to resolving the problem.

This example reflects how high-achievement officers are motivated by competence and contribution rather than reward or status. Their passion is often quiet, their confidence grounded in preparation, and their leadership style based more on influence than authority. Departments that understand these psychological profiles can deploy such officers in ways that maximize impact while nurturing the kind of workplace climate that supports long-term career satisfaction and ethical excellence.

Achievement Under Stress

Stress is an inescapable element of policing. From high-risk traffic stops to emotionally charged domestic incidents, officers are constantly placed in situations that test their decision-making and emotional regulation. The very nature of law enforcement requires composure in the face of uncertainty, the ability to manage competing demands simultaneously, and a capacity to function effectively under scrutiny. For many, these demands can lead to decision fatigue, burnout, or reactive behavior. However, achievement-driven officers often see such stress not as a deterrent but as a challenge to overcome.

High-achievers are often energized by high-stakes environments. Their internal motivation propels them to view crisis situations as opportunities to demonstrate competence and exercise control. They embrace complexity rather than retreat from it, often thriving in dynamic and ambiguous situations where outcomes depend heavily on their choices and performance. Their sense of fulfillment is not found in avoiding mistakes, but in executing solutions. In these environments, they remain highly focused, drawing on both training and intuition to guide their actions.

According to research by Cooper, Davidson, and Robinson (1982), officers with high intrinsic motivation demonstrate better coping mechanisms during acute stress incidents. They tend to appraise situations as problems to be solved rather than threats to be avoided. This aligns with McClelland's findings that high nAch individuals prefer situations where they can exert personal control over outcomes. These officers are more likely to engage in active coping strategies—gathering information, coordinating with peers, and applying problem-solving protocols—rather than emotionally disengaging or deflecting responsibility.

However, it is crucial to distinguish achievement motivation from perfectionism or compulsiveness. While both high-achievers and perfectionists strive for excellence, the latter often do so from a place of fear—of failure, criticism, or inadequacy. High-achievers, by contrast, are more resilient and adaptable. In high-stress situations, achievement-motivated officers exhibit goal-oriented thinking, but not at the cost of flexibility. They accept constructive feedback and adjust tactics when needed. Rather than being derailed by mistakes or setbacks, they use such experiences as fuel for growth.

This psychological resilience is one of their greatest assets. They are more likely to maintain emotional control, recover quickly from difficult incidents, and maintain a sense of purpose even when confronted with trauma or adversity. This doesn't make them immune to the psychological costs of policing, but it does give them a stronger foundation for navigating them constructively. In turn, departments that identify and support these individuals—through peer support, debriefings, and leadership roles—can build a culture that prioritizes both performance and psychological health.

Career Growth and Specialization

Career progression in law enforcement is not solely about rank; it is also about role alignment and professional development. Officers with a high need for achievement are naturally drawn to assignments that offer intellectual challenge, autonomy, and opportunities for mastery. They are more likely to pursue specialized roles that provide them with the structure and freedom to perform at a high level, such as investigations, special operations, intelligence units, or training divisions.

These roles appeal to high achievers because they allow them to work on long-term, goal-oriented projects with measurable outcomes. Detectives, for example, often engage in investigations that unfold over weeks or months, requiring sustained focus and independent judgment. SWAT officers or bomb technicians must perfect skills that demand continuous practice and reflection. In each of these specialized roles, performance can be clearly linked to individual initiative and competence—an ideal environment for those with high nAch.

Achievement-oriented officers also tend to be proactive in planning their own development. They seek out mentors, apply for advanced certifications, and invest in educational opportunities outside the department. Their drive for mastery frequently leads them to initiate projects or process improvements that contribute to overall organizational effectiveness. Importantly, they often take on informal leadership roles before receiving formal promotions, mentoring new officers, or modeling best practices in the field.

A study by Johnson and Button (2000) showed that officers who identify as high achievers report greater job satisfaction and career commitment when placed in roles aligned with their internal motivations. Misalignment, by contrast, can result in frustration, withdrawal, or turnover. Departments that ignore the motivational orientation of their personnel risk losing some of their most talented officers to burnout or career stagnation.

Assessment tools such as the Achievement Motivation Inventory (AMI) can be used to identify officers who are primed for specialized roles or leadership tracks. When paired with structured career planning and individualized development plans, these tools offer a strategic advantage in building a workforce that is both competent and committed. Additionally, transparent promotional processes that reward competence, initiative, and problem-solving—rather than seniority alone—can further reinforce a culture of achievement.

Ultimately, high-achieving officers are not just assets in specialized assignments—they are catalysts for innovation, professional excellence, and cultural transformation within policing. Recognizing and supporting their career trajectories is an investment in both agency performance and public trust.

Practical Implications

Understanding and harnessing achievement motivation within police departments has significant operational and organizational implications. When leadership intentionally integrates motivational psychology into workforce planning, the result is a more resilient, effective, and purpose-driven agency. Below are key areas where practical applications of McClelland's Achievement Motivation Theory can directly impact departmental outcomes:

Recruitment and Promotion: Departments should consider motivation assessments as part of the selection process for leadership or specialized units. Traditional recruitment practices often emphasize physical ability, educational attainment, and past performance. While these are important, they may not fully capture an officer's potential for excellence in roles that require intrinsic drive and independent problem-solving. Tools such as structured interviews, achievement-oriented personality assessments (e.g., AMI), and scenario-based evaluations can help identify candidates with a high need for achievement. Incorporating motivation profiling into promotion decisions ensures that leadership pipelines are filled with individuals who are driven not by power or prestige, but by the desire to make a meaningful impact.

Training and Development: Achievement-oriented officers benefit from training programs that challenge them cognitively and physically while providing clear feedback and measurable outcomes. These officers are not passive participants in learning environments—they thrive on feedback, goal-setting, and opportunities for skill refinement. Training curricula that incorporate problem-based learning, case simulations, and structured evaluations help sustain their engagement. Instructors can also tap into their motivation by assigning leadership roles in training scenarios or offering optional advanced modules that reward initiative. Such targeted development not only improves individual capabilities but also sets a performance standard that can elevate the entire agency.

Assignment Matching: Not all officers are equally suited for all roles. Departments that match motivation profiles with assignments are likely to see improvements in performance, morale, and team dynamics. High-achievers tend to prefer roles that offer autonomy, complexity, and a direct connection between effort and outcome. Examples include detective work, K-9 units, cybercrime investigations, training divisions, and internal affairs. By contrast, officers with a higher need for affiliation may thrive in community policing roles that emphasize relationship-building. Aligning assignments with motivational profiles helps ensure that officers are not just qualified—but fulfilled—by the work they are doing. This also reduces the risk of burnout, disciplinary issues, and performance deterioration.

Mentorship Programs: High-achievers can serve as mentors to newer officers, creating a culture of excellence and upward mobility without relying solely on rank structure. Because high-achieving officers often lead by example and hold themselves to high standards, they are natural role models in peer mentoring settings. Structured mentorship programs that pair experienced high-nAch officers with recruits or early-career officers can help accelerate the professional development of the latter while reinforcing the sense of purpose and contribution in the former. These relationships can also help transmit institutional values, promote ethical behavior, and reduce early attrition by giving younger officers a clear vision of what career success looks like.

In sum, the strategic use of achievement motivation theory can elevate every stage of an officer's career—from hiring to retirement. Departments that understand the psychological composition of their workforce can better design systems of support, accountability, and advancement. As modern policing evolves to meet more complex societal demands, fostering a culture that values internal motivation, ethical excellence, and continuous growth is not just beneficial—it is essential.

Integration with Other Theories of Motivation

While McClelland's Achievement Motivation Theory offers a compelling lens for understanding high-performing officers, its insights are enriched when considered alongside other well-established motivation models—particularly Victor Vroom's Expectancy Theory. Vroom's theory proposes that motivation is a function of three variables: expectancy (the belief that effort leads to performance), instrumentality (the belief that performance leads to outcomes), and valence (the value placed on those outcomes).

For high nAch officers, Vroom's theory helps explain the decision-making process behind their engagement. These individuals are more likely to believe that their personal effort will directly lead to performance outcomes (high expectancy), especially when they have autonomy and control over their assignments. They also perceive a strong link between their high performance and subsequent professional rewards or internal satisfaction (high instrumentality), even if those rewards are intrinsic, such as a sense of mastery or impact. This confidence in their own capabilities reinforces a continuous feedback loop where effort, performance, and reward remain tightly connected.

Moreover, the outcomes sought by high-achievers—personal growth, skill development, recognition by competent peers—carry high valence. These outcomes align closely with their internal goals and sense of identity. In Vroom's framework, this makes them particularly responsive to environments where goal clarity, performance metrics, and feedback mechanisms are robust and transparent. When departments deliver consistent signals that link performance to advancement or esteem, motivation remains high. Conversely, when these cues are inconsistent or absent, even the most driven officers may become frustrated or disengaged (Vroom, 1964).

Vroom's model therefore, complements McClelland by emphasizing the situational contingencies that either enhance or inhibit motivational strength, especially in complex or bureaucratic systems like policing. Where McClelland focuses on the internal psychological drivers—such as the innate need for achievement—Vroom illuminates how organizational systems either enable or block the expression of those drives.

For example, a highly motivated officer may eagerly take on a difficult case (high expectancy), believing it will showcase their skills (instrumentality), and find deep satisfaction in solving it (valence). However, if organizational politics or lack of recognition obscure this process—if their performance is not acknowledged, rewarded, or trusted—they may reduce effort or seek opportunities elsewhere. In this sense, achievement motivation is not only about the individual's disposition, but also about the environment's ability to sustain that drive.

Combining these two theories creates a more holistic understanding of how officers are motivated in practice. It also provides leaders with actionable insight: to sustain high performance, departments must cultivate both the psychological conditions (McClelland, 1961) and the structural incentives (Vroom, 1964) that keep officers engaged. Integrating motivation theory into law enforcement strategy ensures that talent is not only identified but also activated, aligned, and retained over the long term.

Risks and Limitations

While fostering achievement motivation is beneficial, departments should also recognize the potential risks associated with it. High nAch officers can be prone to overextension, especially if they take on excessive responsibilities without institutional support. Their internal drive, if unchecked, may also lead to self-criticism, burnout, or a tendency to bypass team processes in pursuit of personal standards. These officers may operate under the assumption that others should match their intensity, which can inadvertently create tension within teams, especially if leadership fails to balance workloads or establish collective norms.

Additionally, achievement-motivated individuals may prioritize personal success over team cohesion when role expectations or rewards are not carefully managed. In highly competitive or bureaucratic environments, their relentless pursuit of excellence can become isolating, particularly if they perceive peers or supervisors as barriers to goal attainment. Without mechanisms for peer accountability and collaborative engagement, high-achievers may disengage from organizational culture, eroding morale or fostering elitism.

Furthermore, departments that overemphasize achievement motivation risk alienating officers whose core drives lean more toward affiliation or power. Officers motivated by affiliation often prioritize team harmony, community trust, and relationship-building—traits essential to community policing and frontline diplomacy. Those with a strong need for power may gravitate toward leadership, policy influence, or crisis command roles. If departments predominantly reward initiative, speed, or goal completion without honoring contributions rooted in collaboration, loyalty, or strategic vision, they risk reinforcing a narrow definition of excellence.

A balanced workforce strategy should accommodate multiple motivational profiles while leveraging each for appropriate tasks and assignments. Achievement motivation is one pillar of a high-functioning department, but its integration must be thoughtful, inclusive, and adaptive. Recognizing and validating the strengths of officers across the motivational spectrum fosters psychological safety, encourages mutual respect, and creates a richer organizational culture. Ultimately, the goal is not to elevate one style above others, but to orchestrate a dynamic team where every officer's strengths contribute to the collective mission.

Expanded Use of Data and Future Research Directions

Despite the promising insights from McClelland's framework, there remains a need for more empirical data in law enforcement contexts. Future research should explore:

- Correlations between nAch scores and rates of officer advancement or disciplinary action

- Longitudinal studies on burnout rates among high-achieving officers

- Departmental case studies where motivation-based recruitment or training programs were implemented

- Quantitative assessments using tools like the Achievement Motivation Inventory (AMI), combined with performance metrics and retention data, could yield actionable insights for personnel management and training protocols.

Conclusion

The motivational makeup of an officer may determine not only how they perform their duties, but also how long they thrive in service and what kind of legacy they leave. If achievement-driven officers are to be the architects of reform, innovation, and public trust. In that case, departments must do more than deploy them—they must understand, support, and strategically develop them. These officers are not just capable workers; they are often visionaries in uniform, driven by a personal commitment to excellence that exceeds institutional expectations. Departments that cultivate these individuals stand to gain not only performance outcomes but also cultural transformation.

The application of McClelland's Achievement Motivation Theory in law enforcement provides a vital lens through which to view officer behavior, decision-making, and career progression. By identifying and nurturing the achievement-driven officer, departments can build a resilient, high-performing workforce that not only meets the challenges of modern policing but thrives under them. These officers bring an invaluable mix of persistence, accountability, and ethical orientation to their roles—qualities that are increasingly essential in a time of heightened public scrutiny and rapidly evolving community needs.

High-achievement officers are often the quiet drivers of progress in police organizations. Their intrinsic motivation compels them to improve systems, master complex challenges, and uphold high standards even when no one is watching. These individuals do not need extrinsic rewards to maintain performance; rather, they are fueled by the satisfaction of growth, impact, and responsibility. In moments of crisis or institutional change, their presence can stabilize morale, set professional benchmarks, and model adaptive leadership.

Yet as powerful as their internal motivation is, it requires the right environment to flourish. This means creating systems that align professional development with personal growth, structuring leadership pipelines that reward not just longevity but initiative, and reinforcing a culture where purpose is as valued as productivity. When agencies fail to create such environments, they risk squandering the very potential that could lead to lasting reform.

In the broader pursuit of legitimacy, accountability, and reform, motivation remains a foundational concept. Agencies that focus solely on procedures and policies without considering the psychological factors influencing behavior risk addressing symptoms without remedying root causes. Officers who are internally driven to achieve are more likely to seek ethical excellence, contribute to organizational innovation, and embody the core values of service. They act not from fear of punishment or desire for reward, but from a deep sense of duty and competence.

Understanding what motivates officers is not merely an academic exercise—it is a roadmap for sustainable, purpose-driven policing. Departments that prioritize motivational fit during recruitment, challenge high-achievers through meaningful roles, and support them with feedback and development opportunities create not only better officers, but better outcomes for the communities they serve. In this way, achievement motivation becomes more than a theoretical concept—it becomes a strategic asset for building modern, trusted, and effective law enforcement agencies.

What would policing look like if every officer were developed not just for compliance, but for purpose? And how can departments reimagine leadership structures to better align with intrinsic motivation? These are not abstract reflections—they are the essential questions facing police agencies as they prepare for the future. The answers will shape the ethos of public safety for decades to come.

Chapter 3: Detectives vs. Patrol Officers: Autonomy, Complexity, and Purpose

Introduction

In any law enforcement organization, the roles of patrol officers and detectives represent two of the most critical operational functions. These two positions form the backbone of both immediate response and long-term investigation—the frontline defenders and the analytical solvers. While both serve the public interest in safety and justice, the nature of their daily tasks, decision-making demands, and interactions with the community are starkly different. Patrol officers often operate in unpredictable, high-stress environments where quick judgment and presence of mind are essential. Their work demands vigilance, adaptability, and a wide range of interpersonal skills as they interact with citizens in crisis, enforce laws in real time, and maintain a visible presence in the community.

Detectives, in contrast, engage in methodical, time-intensive efforts aimed at uncovering deeper truths behind criminal incidents. Their work involves evidence collection, interviewing, collaboration with legal professionals, and the sustained application of critical thinking. The rhythms of detective work are slower, but the stakes are no less significant. Whereas patrol officers often manage the immediacy of events, detectives manage their complexity. These distinctions are not simply operational—they reflect fundamentally different psychological environments that appeal to different kinds of motivations.

These differences, when viewed through the lens of McClelland's Achievement Motivation Theory, offer profound insights into how officers experience satisfaction, purpose, and effectiveness within their respective roles. By exploring the alignment between motivational needs—achievement, affiliation, and power—and the intrinsic demands of these positions, we can better understand how role fit influences performance, well-being, and long-term commitment to service. Rather than viewing these assignments as interchangeable or transitional, this chapter considers them as domains of specialized engagement where motivational theory can guide recruitment, retention, and development strategies for a more purpose-driven and high-performing workforce.

Distinct Roles, Distinct Motivations

Patrol officers are the frontline of police visibility and the public face of law enforcement. Their responsibilities include responding to emergency calls, conducting traffic stops, patrolling neighborhoods, deterring crime through presence, and managing a wide range of incidents that occur spontaneously. This work is inherently dynamic and reactive, requiring quick decision-making, emotional regulation, and a capacity to switch focus under pressure. Patrol officers must be generalists—equipped to manage everything from domestic disturbances and mental health crises to traffic collisions and violent crimes, often with limited information and under significant time constraints (Chappell & Lanza-Kaduce, 2010).

Detectives, by contrast, perform specialized and methodical functions that emphasize analysis, persistence, and cognitive complexity. Their tasks unfold over days, weeks, or even months, requiring in-depth interviews, evidence collection, surveillance, collaboration with forensic specialists, and close coordination with prosecutors. Detectives rely less on physical presence and more on procedural knowledge, intuition, and deductive reasoning. While their work may lack the constant variety of patrol, it offers depth, continuity, and a clearly defined goal: case resolution (Brown, 1988).

McClelland's (1961) Achievement Motivation Theory offers a useful framework to understand how different individuals are drawn to these contrasting roles. High-achievement motivation (nAch) individuals are intrinsically driven to excel, seek moderately challenging tasks, and derive satisfaction from accomplishments that result from their own efforts. Detectives typically experience these conditions more frequently than patrol officers. Solving a complex case—especially one involving layered evidence, strategic interviewing, and interagency coordination—requires sustained effort, attention to detail, and high cognitive investment. These conditions fulfill the need for achievement by providing delayed but definitive feedback, a sense of personal contribution, and mastery over specialized knowledge areas (Winter, 1991).

Furthermore, detective work supports the autonomy and accountability that high nAch individuals thrive on. They are often granted discretion over investigative priorities, timelines, and tactical decisions. This control enhances motivation and performance, as outlined in job design literature, which emphasizes autonomy as a key determinant of work engagement (Hackman & Oldham, 1976). The satisfaction detectives derive from case resolution aligns directly with McClelland's argument that achievement-oriented individuals seek to influence outcomes through their own capabilities.

Patrol work, while just as vital, engages a different motivational profile. Officers who score higher in the need for affiliation (nAff) may find patrol work fulfilling due to its frequent community interactions, peer collaboration, and engagement in emotionally charged situations. These officers are often effective communicators and empathic listeners, building rapport with victims, witnesses, and community stakeholders. Such traits are especially valuable in community policing models, which emphasize trust-building, visibility, and problem-solving partnerships (Skogan, 2006).

Additionally, the structure of patrol work may appeal to individuals with a high need for power (nPow), particularly those who derive motivation from influencing others or exercising authority. Patrol officers often assume command presence, make on-the-spot legal determinations, and manage complex scenes involving multiple actors. In high-conflict situations—such as crowd control or critical incident response—this form of influence becomes central to restoring order and establishing legitimacy (Engel, 2001).

That said, achievement motivation is still present and valuable in patrol roles. Officers with high nAch may express it through proactive policing—conducting self-initiated stops, pursuing leads without prompts, or mentoring newer recruits. However, the fragmented and often reactive nature of patrol work can limit long-term satisfaction for these individuals unless supplemented by meaningful recognition, discretion, or advancement opportunities. Without visible links between effort and outcome—especially in departments with rigid hierarchies—high nAch officers in patrol may feel underutilized or seek reassignment to more autonomous roles (Ingram et al., 2013).

Understanding these distinctions is vital for departments looking to optimize workforce alignment. Instead of viewing patrol and investigative assignments as merely rotational or hierarchical, leaders should consider them motivationally distinct career tracks. Just as educators differentiate instruction based on student needs, police leaders must differentiate roles based on officer psychology. Doing so enhances morale, improves retention, and enables more effective public service delivery.

Autonomy and Feedback in Job Satisfaction

Job satisfaction remains one of the most studied and strategically important constructs in law enforcement workforce management. Among the many factors influencing officer satisfaction and retention, autonomy and feedback consistently rank as some of the most influential (Brough & Frame, 2004; Tummers & Knies, 2013). Autonomy—the degree to which officers can exercise discretion and make independent decisions—directly supports intrinsic motivation and psychological ownership. Feedback—the quality, frequency, and relevance of performance information—reinforces self-efficacy and contributes to a sense of professional growth.

Detectives, by the nature of their role, are typically granted greater autonomy than their patrol counterparts. They control more of their scheduling, determine investigative priorities, and shape the trajectory of their cases. This case ownership provides them with continuity and depth, allowing them to follow leads, adjust strategies, and see investigations through from inception to closure. In line with self-determination theory (Deci & Ryan, 2000), this form of structured autonomy enhances feelings of competence and purpose, which are foundational to sustained motivation.

Furthermore, feedback for detectives is often tangible and cumulative. Success is measured not just by task completion, but by case outcomes—arrests, confessions, convictions, or recovered assets. While not every investigation leads to closure, the work offers an opportunity to learn from failure, refine techniques, and deepen expertise over time. These iterative cycles of performance and feedback align closely with what McClelland (1961) identified as ideal conditions for high-achievement motivation: goal clarity, individual accountability, and progress evaluation.

In contrast, patrol officers frequently operate under constrained autonomy. Their shifts are dictated by seniority and operational needs. Their calls for service are dispatched with little discretion. They move from incident to incident, rarely seeing the long-term results of their interventions. While this model is essential to ensuring timely response and coverage across jurisdictions, it can reduce feelings of agency and accomplishment—especially for officers driven by achievement needs.

Moreover, feedback in patrol work tends to be immediate but surface-level. Officers may receive praise for prompt response or critique for procedural missteps, but seldom receive a detailed analysis of their long-term impact. A domestic call resolved without incident may receive no formal acknowledgment, while an arrest may trigger a paperwork audit but no discussion of its social or investigative value. This pattern can produce a feedback vacuum, particularly for high nAch officers who desire metrics of improvement and recognition of complexity handled.

Studies by Brough and Frame (2004) and later by Zhao, He, and Lovrich (2002) show that perceived autonomy significantly correlates with job satisfaction and organizational commitment among law enforcement personnel. Officers who feel trusted to exercise judgment, who receive consistent developmental feedback, and who perceive their contributions as valued are more likely to remain engaged and less likely to experience burnout or disillusionment.

The importance of feedback also extends to learning and development. According to London and Smither (2002), feedback is most effective when it is timely, specific, and linked to behavior that can be modified. In detective units, supervisors often hold debriefings and case reviews, offering detailed critiques and opportunities for skill refinement. Patrol supervisors, by contrast, may be constrained by time, call volume, and a more reactive management style, limiting their ability to coach officers in real-time or reflect on cumulative performance.

One promising strategy to mitigate this imbalance is the implementation of structured peer review or after-action reviews in patrol settings. When officers debrief each other after calls, or when field training officers provide real-time coaching, the quality of feedback improves and so does morale. Empowering patrol officers with decision-making discretion—such as allowing flexibility in traffic enforcement, discretionary time for community engagement, or rotating leadership roles during calls—can also strengthen autonomy and enhance motivation.

Departments must recognize that autonomy and feedback are not static traits of a role, but managerial design variables. Even within patrol assignments, creative scheduling, supervisory development, and recognition systems can increase job satisfaction and motivation. Officers who are trusted, listened to, and given room to exercise professional judgment are more likely to invest themselves fully in the mission.

When viewed through McClelland's lens, the takeaway is clear: high nAch officers require a work environment that not only permits but encourages performance ownership and reflective growth. When autonomy and feedback are lacking, these officers may feel stagnated, underutilized, or tempted to pursue alternative assignments or careers. Conversely, when these elements are embedded into the role—regardless of whether one wears a patrol uniform or a detective badge—officers experience their work as meaningful, challenging, and aligned with their personal aspirations.

Aligning Roles with Motivational Profiles

The practical value of understanding motivational profiles in policing lies in its transformative potential for workforce planning, assignment strategy, retention, and leadership development. Every officer brings a unique constellation of personality traits, values, and psychological needs to their role. Recognizing and aligning these internal drivers with the structure and expectations of specific assignments is not just a matter of employee satisfaction—it is a strategic imperative that can enhance operational effectiveness and organizational resilience.

David McClelland's Human Motivation Theory posits that individuals are primarily driven by three core needs: achievement (nAch), power (nPow), and affiliation (nAff). These motivational orientations shape how individuals approach challenges, interact with colleagues, respond to feedback, and derive satisfaction from their work. Matching roles with these motivational profiles can unlock a deeper level of engagement and purpose that no amount of external reward alone can achieve (McClelland, 1961).

High-achievement officers (nAch) are driven by mastery, progress, and the pursuit of excellence. They tend to thrive in roles that offer clear goals, personal accountability, and opportunities to demonstrate competence. Detective divisions, task forces, intelligence units, and analytical crime mapping roles are ideal fits for this group. These assignments allow officers to tackle complex problems, develop long-term strategies, and produce measurable outcomes. High nAch officers are also more likely to benefit from training programs that emphasize performance feedback, problem-solving, and skill development (Winter, 1991).

Conversely, officers with a strong need for power (nPow) are motivated by the opportunity to influence others, assert authority, and effect organizational or community change. These individuals often excel in tactical teams such as SWAT, supervisory and command roles, policy advocacy, and field training positions. Tactical environments, in particular, satisfy nPow officers through leadership under pressure, rapid decision-making, and visible outcomes. They are often energized by high-stakes situations and enjoy leading others toward mission success (Yukl, 2013). As supervisors or trainers, they can transmit organizational values and reinforce cultural standards across generations of officers.

Officers high in the need for affiliation (nAff) find meaning in interpersonal connection, emotional resonance, and collaborative engagement. These officers often flourish in roles that prioritize relationship-building and trust, such as community policing, school resource officer (SRO) positions, victim services, and crisis intervention teams. In these assignments, the goal is not merely enforcement but sustained communication, empathy, and responsiveness. Officers with high nAff are more likely to succeed in de-escalating emotionally charged encounters, building rapport with underserved communities, and contributing to legitimacy in public safety (Skogan, 2006).

The benefits of motivational alignment extend beyond the individual to the organisation as a whole. When officers are assigned to roles that align with their core drives, their levels of motivation, performance, and psychological resilience increase. They are more likely to view their work as meaningful and less likely to experience burnout or turnover. This alignment also reduces disciplinary infractions and conflict, as officers operate in environments that support rather than constrain their strengths (Johnson, 2012).

On the contrary, misalignment can erode morale and productivity. A high nAch officer assigned to a repetitive administrative post may experience frustration and stagnation. An nAff-driven officer placed in a solitary, intelligence-focused role may feel isolated or emotionally depleted. An nPow officer relegated to back-end clerical duties may disengage or become disruptive in pursuit of influence. These mismatches not only reduce individual effectiveness but also create ripple effects in team dynamics, supervision, and public interaction.

To prevent such outcomes, agencies should incorporate motivational profiling into recruitment, performance evaluations, and career development planning. This does not require formal psychological testing in all cases—although tools such as the Achievement Motivation Inventory (AMI) can be helpful—but can involve structured interviews, observation-based assessments, and feedback from training officers. Leaders should be trained to recognize behavioral indicators of motivation type, such as initiative, interpersonal style, risk tolerance, and response to feedback (Goleman, 2006).

In addition to alignment, departments should foster pathways for officers to shift roles as their interests and needs evolve. Motivation is not static; it can shift over the course of a career. An officer who begins with high power needs may later develop a strong drive for affiliation after years in the field. Others may discover a latent achievement drive as they take on new challenges or recover from periods of disengagement. Flexible career tracks, mentoring programs, and rotational assignments can support these transitions and prevent stagnation.

Ultimately, the integration of motivational theory into workforce strategy represents a maturation of police human resource management. It moves departments from a transactional view of personnel—as interchangeable parts—to a developmental view of officers as individuals with unique capacities and aspirations. In doing so, agencies build not just better teams, but a culture of trust, growth, and performance that reflects the full complexity of the communities they serve.

Conclusion

Detectives and patrol officers may share the same badge and organizational mission, but their motivations, satisfiers, and stressors differ significantly. These differences are not merely a function of job description or departmental structure—they are rooted in fundamental psychological profiles that influence how officers perceive their roles, interact with colleagues and communities, and sustain performance over time. By applying McClelland's Achievement Motivation Theory to these roles, law enforcement leaders gain a powerful framework for understanding, predicting, and shaping officer behavior. This understanding allows for more intelligent workforce planning, role assignment, leadership development, and morale management.

Modern policing demands more than just competence—it demands adaptability, resilience, and intrinsic motivation. Officers who feel psychologically aligned with their assignments are more likely to thrive under pressure, form productive relationships, and maintain ethical standards even in high-stress situations. Recognizing the unique motivational contours of patrol officers and detectives helps leaders avoid the pitfalls of role misalignment, such as disengagement, burnout, or disciplinary incidents, and instead fosters environments that cultivate excellence and well-being.

In particular, achievement-motivated officers (nAch) benefit from roles that offer autonomy, measurable goals, and long-term feedback—conditions more commonly found in investigative, analytical, or leadership-track assignments. Conversely, those motivated by affiliation (nAff) or power (nPow) can make extraordinary contributions in community-facing roles, tactical units, or supervisory capacities where interpersonal influence or relationship-building are critical. By aligning these motivational needs with organizational roles, departments can increase productivity, lower attrition, and reinforce a culture of trust and professionalism.

Creating a culture where motivation is not only understood but actively managed enables departments to evolve beyond one-size-fits-all deployment. It transforms human resource management from a reactive process to a strategic discipline. Purpose-driven policing emerges when officers are placed where they perform best, grow most, and serve with the greatest impact. This approach is particularly vital as departments confront growing public scrutiny, mental health crises within the force, and the challenge of retaining a skilled and diverse workforce.

Moreover, applying motivation theory at the organizational level encourages a shift from compliance-based management to development-based leadership. Rather than relying solely on policies and procedures to shape behavior, departments that embrace psychological insights foster environments where officers are intrinsically committed to doing their best work. This shift supports long-term reform goals by embedding accountability, ethical reasoning, and professional pride into the daily fabric of policing.

Understanding and leveraging motivational diversity also positions departments to better support equity and inclusion. Officers from different backgrounds may enter the profession with varied life experiences and value systems. Recognizing that there is no single pathway to effective service allows departments to craft diverse teams that reflect the communities they serve—not just demographically, but motivationally. This inclusive mindset strengthens legitimacy and fosters community trust.

Ultimately, this chapter highlights the importance of moving beyond generic performance models and instead embracing a nuanced, evidence-based understanding of what drives officers in different roles. The detective who solves a case after months of investigation and the patrol officer who de-escalates a volatile encounter with empathy are both expressions of excellence—but they emerge from different motivational roots. Honoring that distinction is not only respectful—it is strategic.

In the evolving landscape of 21st-century law enforcement, success will belong to agencies that invest not just in tools and tactics, but in people and purpose. McClelland's framework, and motivational theory more broadly, offer not just academic insight but practical guidance for building departments that are resilient, ethical, and aligned. The future of policing depends not on uniformity, but on understanding. And in that understanding lies the blueprint for lasting change.

Chapter 4:
Measuring What Matters: The Achievement Motivation Inventory (AMI) and Beyond

Introduction

Understanding what motivates law enforcement officers requires more than anecdotal insight or observational assessments. While traditional performance metrics such as arrests, response times, or complaints offer surface-level evaluations of behavior, they fall short of revealing the deeper psychological drivers that shape an officer's choices, persistence, and engagement over time. Motivation operates beneath observable conduct—it is the internal compass that orients effort, defines success, and sustains energy in the face of adversity. In high-stakes fields like policing, where split-second decisions, chronic stress, and evolving community expectations are the norm, understanding this internal compass is essential for cultivating a resilient, ethical, and high-performing workforce.

In the realm of evidence-based policing and psychological science, psychometric tools offer a standardized, validated way to assess these internal drivers. Unlike unstructured interviews or informal supervisor appraisals, which are often subject to bias, inconsistency, and situational distortion, psychometric instruments rely on statistically reliable methods to measure specific psychological constructs. These tools allow researchers and practitioners to evaluate traits such as need for achievement, tolerance for ambiguity, preference for autonomy, or interpersonal orientation with rigor and repeatability.

This scientific approach to personnel assessment has gained traction in law enforcement as departments seek to professionalize their recruitment and retention strategies, improve leadership pipelines, and respond to increasing public demands for transparency and accountability. By measuring motivation directly, departments can better predict who will thrive in different roles, adapt to stress, and remain committed over the long haul. It also allows for early identification of officers who may need developmental support, realignment, or mentoring to avoid burnout or disengagement.

Among the most comprehensive and academically grounded tools for assessing achievement-related motivation is the **Achievement Motivation Inventory (AMI)**, developed by Schuler and Prochaska (2001). Unlike generic personality tests, the AMI was explicitly designed to parse out the nuanced facets of achievement motivation—one of the most critical drivers of performance in high-reliability occupations such as law enforcement, aviation, and emergency medicine. Its multidimensional structure enables a far more detailed motivational profile than traditional tests like the Myers-Briggs Type Indicator (MBTI) or even the Big Five personality traits, which focus more broadly on temperament and behavioral style.

The AMI evaluates 17 distinct facets of achievement motivation, including traits such as competitiveness, confidence in success, goal setting, preference for difficult tasks, persistence, eagerness to learn, and internality—the belief that one's outcomes are determined by personal actions rather than external forces. These dimensions are not only theoretically sound but also practically useful for aligning personnel with appropriate assignments, identifying leadership potential, and shaping customized training interventions.

For law enforcement professionals, the value of such a granular assessment cannot be overstated. Consider the contrasting demands of a homicide detective and a community liaison officer. The former requires long-term persistence, a preference for complexity, and high internal control, while the latter may succeed through empathy, social adaptability, and affiliation motivation. The AMI helps distinguish between these profiles with clarity and empirical validity.

Furthermore, the AMI's structure lends itself to both individual assessment and organizational analysis. It can be used to develop psychological benchmarks for specialized units, track the impact of leadership programs over time, or conduct agency-wide climate assessments regarding motivational fit. Departments that invest in these tools gain not only a clearer picture of their workforce but also a roadmap for sustainable human capital development.

The application of the AMI also aligns well with David McClelland's (1961) foundational theory of human motivation, which identifies achievement (nAch), power (nPow), and affiliation (nAff) as the core drivers of human behavior. The AMI refines this theoretical model by breaking down nAch into component traits and offering an operational framework for measurement. In doing so, it bridges the gap between psychological theory and field-based practice—a critical step for agencies committed to evidence-informed decision-making.

Beyond recruitment and assignment, motivation assessments like the AMI can also play a role in officer wellness and retention. By identifying motivational misfit—such as high nAch officers stuck in low-autonomy, high-bureaucracy roles—agencies can intervene before dissatisfaction metastasizes into burnout, misconduct, or attrition. It also empowers officers to take greater ownership of their career development by fostering self-awareness and aligning personal aspirations with organizational pathways.

In this way, the AMI and similar tools provide not just insight, but leverage—helping departments not only understand who their officers are but also guide them toward becoming who they could be. As such, these instruments serve as essential bridges between psychology and policy, between the individual and the institution, between theory and practice.

The AMI and related tools provide a foundation for integrating motivation science into law enforcement recruitment, development, and organizational research. Their value lies not only in what they measure, but also in how they enable departments to evolve: toward more humane, strategic, and responsive personnel systems that recognize the central role of motivation in achieving policing excellence.

The Achievement Motivation Inventory (AMI): Structure and Relevance

The Achievement Motivation Inventory (AMI), developed by Heinz Schuler and Michael Prochaska (2001), is one of the most comprehensive tools available for measuring the multidimensional construct of achievement motivation. Unlike single-score assessments that offer a broad or generalized measure of motivation, the AMI breaks achievement motivation into 17 distinct facets, offering a rich, nuanced understanding of the ways individuals pursue goals, overcome challenges, and perceive success.

The 17 facets include: (1) persistence, (2) dominance, (3) eagerness to learn, (4) flow, (5) flexibility, (6) fearlessness, (7) status orientation, (8) internality, (9) preference for difficult tasks, (10) self-control, (11) confidence in success, (12) goal setting, (13) compensatory effort, (14) pride in productivity, (15) competitiveness, (16) engagement, and (17) independence. Each of these dimensions reflects a different psychological aspect of achievement behavior. For example, "persistence" measures an individual's tendency to remain committed despite setbacks, while "preference for difficult tasks" reflects their willingness to tackle complex or high-stakes challenges. "Internality" assesses the extent to which individuals attribute their outcomes to their own actions versus external factors—a core indicator of proactive coping and self-responsibility.

The AMI is a self-report inventory composed of 170 items, typically requiring 30 to 40 minutes to complete. Respondents rate their agreement with various statements on a Likert-type scale. The inventory can be administered in both paper-based and digital formats, which makes it adaptable for use in academic studies, recruitment settings, and organizational development programs. Scoring yields both a global achievement motivation score and individual subscale scores, enabling a multi-layered interpretation of an individual's motivational profile.

The relevance of the AMI to law enforcement settings is significant. Law enforcement officers operate in environments characterized by high stress, shifting priorities, and complex interpersonal demands. Their ability to thrive often depends on traits such as persistence, self-control, confidence in success, and internality. Officers high in persistence are likely to remain engaged in protracted investigations or long shifts without losing focus. Those who score highly on goal setting and confidence in success are often proactive problem-solvers, ideal for roles that require initiative and independent decision-making, such as field supervision or specialty task forces.

Conversely, low scores in flexibility or fearlessness might indicate difficulty adjusting to dynamic field conditions or a heightened risk aversion that could impair decision-making during emergencies. Similarly, status orientation—while valuable for some leadership positions—might correlate with unhealthy competition or dominance in team settings if not moderated by emotional intelligence or affiliation motivation.

The AMI's multidimensional format provides law enforcement agencies with a tool to better match officers to roles that align with their intrinsic motivational structures. For example, officers with high scores in "preference for difficult tasks," "eagerness to learn," and "independence" might excel in detective or forensic roles, where ambiguity, intellectual challenge, and self-direction are critical. On the other hand, those scoring higher on "flow," "affiliation," or "flexibility" might find fulfillment in community policing roles that demand emotional intelligence, interpersonal rapport, and contextual adaptability.

Moreover, the AMI supports leadership development by identifying traits associated with high-potential candidates. Officers who demonstrate high "goal setting," "dominance," and "confidence in success" may be strong candidates for promotional tracks, provided they also exhibit balance in areas like "flexibility" and "internality," which correlate with ethical reasoning and resilience under stress. Departments can use these profiles to tailor development programs, coaching strategies, and mentorship assignments, thereby investing in officer growth in a personalized, data-driven manner.

From a theoretical standpoint, the AMI builds upon and operationalizes McClelland's (1961) core motivation theory, especially the concept of nAch—need for achievement. McClelland argued that individuals with high nAch are intrinsically motivated by mastery, excellence, and challenge. The AMI extends this by identifying what kinds of achievement-related behaviors are most prominent in a given individual. For instance, two officers might both be high in nAch, but one may express it through competitiveness and dominance, while the other shows it through independence and persistence. Understanding these subtypes helps departments move beyond simplistic "high vs. low" motivation labels and engage with officer development on a more granular level.

Furthermore, because the AMI has been normed across multiple occupational groups and validated through decades of research, it possesses strong psychometric properties, including internal consistency, construct validity, and predictive utility. This makes it an appropriate tool not only for academic research but for field-based organizational assessments where reliability is crucial. As policing becomes more data-driven, the integration of scientifically grounded tools like the AMI into human resources and training decisions can elevate the professionalism and effectiveness of personnel systems.

In short, the AMI provides an unparalleled framework for dissecting the complex motivational landscape of law enforcement professionals. It brings the rigor of psychological science to the practice of police management and offers a path toward more strategic, individualized, and ethical workforce development. As departments confront increasing pressures to improve performance, transparency, and wellness, the AMI stands out as a critical instrument for measuring—and managing—what truly matters.

Complementary and Alternative Tools

While the Achievement Motivation Inventory (AMI) remains a gold standard for assessing achievement motivation, it is not the only psychometric tool available to organizations aiming to understand and develop their workforce. A variety of complementary and alternative instruments offer unique perspectives on motivation, talent, and individual differences. These tools can be particularly useful when integrated into a broader assessment strategy, offering cross-validation and multidimensional insights into officer behavior and job fit. Below is an overview of several commonly used instruments and their relevance to law enforcement settings.

The Work Preference Inventory (WPI), developed by Amabile, Hill, Hennessey, and Tighe (1994), the WPI assesses two fundamental types of motivation: intrinsic and extrinsic. Intrinsic motivation is driven by internal satisfaction and personal interest, whereas extrinsic motivation stems from external rewards such as salary, recognition, or promotion. The WPI is particularly useful in law enforcement settings to identify whether officers are more likely to engage in tasks for the inherent satisfaction of service or in anticipation of rewards. Officers with high intrinsic motivation may be more resilient to organizational stress and less reliant on external validation, making them ideal for roles that require sustained, independent effort—such as investigations or cold case analysis. On the other hand, those with stronger extrinsic orientation may be more motivated in environments that offer frequent performance evaluations, structured promotions, or public recognition.

The Motivational Sources Inventory (MSI): Barbuto and Scholl (1998) developed the MSI to measure five sources of motivation: intrinsic process, instrumental, external self-concept, internal self-concept, and goal internalization. These sources offer a more nuanced categorization than traditional models and are closely aligned with McClelland's needs for achievement, power, and affiliation. In law enforcement contexts, the MSI can help identify which officers are motivated by service to a cause (goal internalization), the desire to conform to external standards (external self-concept), or internal values and standards (internal self-concept). This is particularly valuable in environments where team cohesion, ethical integrity, and leadership credibility are critical. For example, identifying officers with high internal self-concept motivation could inform the selection of field training officers or ethics liaisons who serve as role models within the department.

CliftonStrengths (StrengthsFinder) CliftonStrengths, developed by the Gallup Organization, is not a traditional motivational assessment but a strengths-based inventory that identifies an individual's top talent themes across domains such as strategic thinking, relationship building, influencing, and execution. While not rooted in a specific motivational theory, the CliftonStrengths tool is widely used in leadership development and team building. Its relevance in law enforcement lies in its ability to map natural talent to role-specific demands. For example, an officer high in the "Analytical" and "Responsibility" themes might thrive in policy review or internal affairs, while one scoring highly in "Command" and "Communication" may be suited for crisis negotiation or community outreach. Although not diagnostic of motivation per se, CliftonStrengths supports the broader goal of motivational alignment by showing how officers prefer to operate and where they can most meaningfully contribute.

Self-Determination Scales (e.g., Basic Psychological Needs Scale) Derived from Deci and Ryan's (2000) Self-Determination Theory (SDT), tools such as the Basic Psychological Needs Scale measure three fundamental psychological needs: autonomy, competence, and relatedness. These needs are seen as essential for intrinsic motivation and psychological well-being. In law enforcement, where rigid hierarchies and operational stress can diminish feelings of autonomy or relatedness, SDT-based tools offer valuable insight into wellness, morale, and engagement. For instance, an officer who reports low autonomy and high burnout might benefit from reassignment to a more autonomous role or from increased participatory decision-making. SDT assessments are particularly relevant in wellness programs, peer support initiatives, and departmental climate studies.

Comparative Considerations: Each of these tools offers specific strengths and potential limitations. The WPI excels in distinguishing motivational types but lacks the granularity of the AMI in terms of achievement facets. The MSI offers rich conceptual alignment with McClelland's theory, but it requires careful interpretation and the guidance of trained facilitators. CliftonStrengths provides accessible language and developmental framing but does not directly measure motivation. Self-determination scales provide robust insight into wellness and engagement, but may lack job-specific applicability without customization.

Therefore, the selection of the appropriate tool must be guided by the research question, population characteristics, and operational context. In high-risk, high-stakes environments like policing, assessments must be validated for use with frontline personnel, resilient to social desirability bias, and administered with attention to confidentiality and psychological safety. Furthermore, cultural competence is essential—both in the construction of assessment items and in their interpretation. Motivational constructs do not operate in a vacuum; they are shaped by culture, gender, experience, and occupational identity.

When used thoughtfully and in combination, these tools can enrich our understanding of what drives police officers—how they find meaning, how they sustain performance, and how they might grow. Psychometric assessment thus becomes not only a tool for diagnosis, but a platform for empowerment, guiding officers and organizations alike toward greater alignment and excellence.

Applying Psychometrics in Law Enforcement Research

Psychometric assessments like the Achievement Motivation Inventory (AMI) are most powerful when used not in isolation, but as part of a broader organizational or academic research agenda. Their true potential lies in triangulating motivation data with other performance, behavioral, and organizational indicators to generate comprehensive insights that inform personnel decisions, leadership development, and agency-wide reform initiatives.

In practical terms, psychometric tools have been successfully integrated into various facets of law enforcement administration. These include leadership development programs, workforce capability assessments, psychological fitness-for-duty evaluations, and promotional screening processes. For example, when incorporated into a department's command school curriculum, tools like the AMI can help identify candidates with strong internality, persistence, and goal orientation—traits that often translate into effective, ethical, and consistent leadership.

In recruitment, psychometrics can help departments move beyond superficial indicators of potential (e.g., physical fitness or test scores) and instead evaluate whether a candidate possesses the motivational resilience and problem-solving orientation suited for the rigors of modern policing. Similarly, in pre-transfer evaluations, motivational inventories can be used to match officers with roles that best fit their achievement profiles, such as transitioning a highly goal-oriented patrol officer into an investigative or administrative role.

In academic research, motivation metrics provide an invaluable means of investigating the relationship between personality traits and real-world outcomes. Studies can explore correlations between motivational profiles and a range of variables, including the number of complaints, frequency of commendations, disciplinary infractions, sick leave usage, voluntary turnover, performance ratings, and promotion velocity. These metrics not only illuminate the psychological underpinnings of effective policing but also help agencies benchmark the qualities associated with success in specific roles or under particular conditions.

The literature increasingly supports the predictive validity of motivation assessments in policing contexts. For instance, Brough and Frame (2004) demonstrated that motivational constructs like self-efficacy and goal clarity were significant predictors of job satisfaction and organizational commitment among Australian police officers. Their findings suggest that fostering a motivationally aligned workforce is not only a psychological goal but an operational imperative. Similarly, Johnson (2012) emphasized that individual motivational profiles—particularly those associated with the need for achievement—are linked to stronger organizational loyalty and enhanced occupational resilience, particularly in high-stress environments.

Additional research by Jex and Bliese (1999) has shown that when motivation is aligned with the job role and supervisory support is present, officers demonstrate improved stress coping, lower burnout rates, and more adaptive engagement patterns. These findings reinforce the idea that motivation is not merely a fixed trait but an interactive process shaped by the work environment, leadership style, and perceived opportunity for growth.

To maximize the utility of psychometric data, assessments must be analyzed in conjunction with relevant contextual variables. These include factors such as rank, assignment type, years of service, educational background, exposure to critical incidents, shift schedules, and unit culture. For example, the same motivational trait—such as high competitiveness—may manifest positively in tactical team environments but become a liability in community liaison roles if not moderated by affiliation needs.

Furthermore, the integration of motivation assessments with 360-degree feedback systems, supervisor evaluations, and peer reviews can create a more holistic personnel development framework. This triangulated approach ensures that motivational data is not viewed in a vacuum but interpreted alongside interpersonal competencies, observed behavior, and operational outcomes. It can also foster a culture of self-awareness and continuous improvement, where officers are encouraged to understand and leverage their strengths while receiving targeted coaching in areas of growth.

Beyond internal operations, psychometric research can also inform broader public policy. For example, departments engaged in consent decrees or reform mandates can use motivation assessments to track cultural shifts over time, monitor the impact of new training initiatives, or identify resistance to change. In such cases, psychometrics function as both diagnostic and evaluative tools, providing a longitudinal lens on reform progress.

Finally, ethical considerations must guide all research applications. Officers must be fully informed about the nature of the assessments, assured of confidentiality, and given access to their results when appropriate. Data should be used for developmental—not punitive—purposes, and interpretations should be grounded in both scientific validity and practical compassion.

In sum, the application of psychometrics in law enforcement research represents a powerful, evidence-based strategy for building organizational capacity, enhancing individual performance, and fostering a culture of psychological insight and ethical growth. When implemented responsibly, motivation assessments like the AMI can transform data into strategy—and strategy into sustainable public service excellence.

Ethical and Practical Considerations

The use of motivation assessments in law enforcement is not without ethical challenges. As these tools gain traction in recruitment, leadership development, and organizational diagnostics, departments must be vigilant in ensuring that their application aligns with the values of fairness, transparency, and psychological safety. The first and most pressing concern is the issue of informed consent. Officers should be made fully aware of the nature, purpose, and potential uses of the assessments they are being asked to complete. Participation should be voluntary whenever possible, and in cases where it is required (e.g., for leadership development), officers must receive assurances about how the data will be handled and protected. Clear communication that the tools are intended for developmental rather than punitive purposes is essential to securing buy-in and reducing resistance.

Confidentiality is another cornerstone of ethical assessment. Personal motivational data must be stored securely, accessed only by qualified personnel, and used solely for the purposes outlined in advance. Without these safeguards, assessments can erode trust, particularly in departments already grappling with morale issues or historical abuses of personnel data. Furthermore, if officers believe their responses could negatively influence promotions, assignments, or disciplinary decisions, they may respond defensively or dishonestly, undermining the reliability of the tool and the legitimacy of the process.

A second ethical issue is the risk of motivational profiling being used to unfairly limit advancement or pigeonhole officers into narrow roles. For instance, if an officer scores low on competitiveness or dominance, it would be unethical to automatically exclude them from leadership tracks without considering their other strengths or contextual factors. Human behavior is dynamic and influenced by experience, environment, and personal growth. Assessments should inform—not dictate—personnel decisions. Departments must be trained not only in how to interpret results, but also in how to incorporate them as one data point within a broader, holistic decision-making framework. Rigidity in application can lead to demoralization, missed talent, and even legal liabilities if perceived as discriminatory.

Third, cultural, gender, and racial biases embedded in psychometric instruments must be proactively addressed. Many widely used tools were developed in Western, predominantly white, and non-policing samples, raising questions about their cross-cultural validity and relevance in diverse law enforcement populations. Motivation itself may be shaped by cultural norms—such as collectivism versus individualism—that influence how officers interpret questions and express their goals. For example, an officer from a collectivist culture may underreport assertiveness or preference for autonomy not because they lack motivation, but because their values emphasize harmony and group alignment.

To mitigate such risks, departments should prioritize tools that have been normed on diverse samples or conduct their own local validation studies to assess how instruments perform in their specific operational environment. Items that show differential functioning across demographic groups should be revised or eliminated. Interpretation of results should also be sensitive to cultural meaning and contextual pressures. An officer's motivational profile may reflect not only internal traits but also adaptive strategies to workplace norms, leadership expectations, or prior experiences with bias.

Practical considerations are equally important. The administration of motivational assessments requires time, trained personnel, and appropriate infrastructure. Officers must be given sufficient time to complete instruments without undue stress or interruption. Those tasked with interpreting results should have training in psychological assessment or work closely with industrial-organizational psychologists to avoid misapplication. Feedback should be delivered constructively and privately, with an emphasis on development and self-awareness rather than judgment.

Another practical issue is the integration of motivation assessments with other systems. For example, aligning assessment findings with performance reviews, mentorship programs, or individualized training plans requires organizational coordination and a culture that values long-term development over short-term metrics. Without such alignment, assessments may become siloed, underutilized, or viewed as burdensome rather than beneficial.

Finally, departments must evaluate the return on investment of implementing psychometric assessments. While the long-term benefits of enhanced job fit, reduced turnover, and improved morale are substantial, initial costs for training, licensing, and integration may be high. Pilot programs, data collection, and feedback loops should be built into the rollout process to ensure continuous improvement and adaptation to organizational needs.

In conclusion, motivation assessments offer powerful insights into law enforcement personnel, but their ethical and practical implementation requires careful planning, inclusive design, and a commitment to fairness. When deployed thoughtfully, these tools can help build more motivated, self-aware, and strategically aligned police forces. When misused or poorly managed, they risk becoming instruments of mistrust and inequity. Departments must proceed not only with scientific rigor but also with moral clarity and organizational transparency.

Case Study: A Municipal Motivation Survey

In 2023, a midsized municipal police department in the southeastern United States partnered with a local university to conduct a groundbreaking pilot study using the Achievement Motivation Inventory (AMI) among 78 sworn officers. The initiative was part of a broader organizational development strategy aimed at aligning personnel decisions with evidence-based insights into motivation, performance, and leadership potential. The research was designed collaboratively between police leadership, human resources, and faculty in industrial-organizational psychology, with institutional review board (IRB) oversight to ensure ethical data collection and confidentiality.

The primary goals of the study were threefold:

1. Identify motivational trends across patrol, investigative, and administrative divisions;

2. Correlate motivational profiles with job satisfaction, disciplinary history, peer and supervisory ratings;

3. Inform future training curricula, assignment practices, and mentorship strategies.

The AMI was administered electronically over a two-week period during designated professional development hours. Officers were briefed about the purpose of the study, assured of anonymity, and provided with individualized summaries of their motivational profiles. Data analysis focused on cross-sectional trends as well as exploratory correlations with personnel data.

Preliminary findings revealed several patterns that aligned with expectations but also offered new insights. Detectives scored highest on persistence, internality, and preference for difficult tasks—traits highly compatible with investigative work that requires long-term focus, autonomy, and strategic problem-solving. These officers also tended to score lower on fear of failure and higher on confidence in success, suggesting a strong sense of efficacy and psychological resilience.

Patrol officers, by contrast, demonstrated elevated scores in dominance, competitiveness, and status orientation. These traits were interpreted as adaptive responses to the immediate, high-stakes, and public-facing nature of patrol duties. High dominance scores correlated with assertiveness in decision-making and comfort with hierarchical structures—important attributes for managing unpredictable encounters in the field. However, some officers in this group scored lower on goal setting and compensatory effort, indicating potential disengagement or motivational misalignment, particularly among those with more than 10 years of service and no recent reassignment.

Administrative personnel, including sergeants and civilian liaisons, exhibited stronger preferences for order, planning, and goal structure. These findings reflected the bureaucratic demands of the roles, which require long-term coordination, policy adherence, and process management. Interestingly, administrative staff who scored low on internality were more likely to report frustration with decision-making processes, suggesting that enhancing their role clarity and input in department-wide planning could improve job satisfaction.

A particularly noteworthy result was the correlation between high scores in "confidence in success" and favorable behavioral outcomes. Officers in this category had the fewest disciplinary actions, received the most peer commendations, and scored highest in 360-degree evaluations. This supported earlier research (e.g., Brough & Frame, 2004; Johnson, 2012) indicating that self-efficacy and positive expectancy beliefs are critical in policing performance and professionalism.

The study's implications were immediate and far-reaching. Based on the findings, the department implemented several initiatives:

- A voluntary mentoring program was launched, matching high nAch officers with probationary recruits during their field training period. These mentors focused not only on skills transfer but on helping new officers develop goal clarity and adaptive motivational strategies.

- Leadership training modules were revised to incorporate motivational theory, encouraging supervisors to identify and engage the motivational profiles of their subordinates during evaluations, team assignments, and disciplinary proceedings.

- Promotional processes were adjusted to include AMI-informed developmental feedback. Officers applying for specialized or command roles received summary reports that highlighted strengths and areas for growth based on their motivational patterns, fostering a culture of self-awareness and continuous improvement.

Feedback from participants was overwhelmingly positive. Officers expressed appreciation for receiving structured insight into their own professional drivers, with several noting that the process helped them reframe career aspirations or re-engage with departmental opportunities. Supervisors reported improved coaching conversations, enhanced morale in units where motivational alignment was prioritized, and greater enthusiasm for collaborative projects.

From a research perspective, the project was considered a success, and plans were made to expand the study in the following fiscal year to include dispatch personnel, tactical teams, and school resource officers. The university partner also received a grant to analyze longitudinal outcomes such as retention, promotion, and wellness indicators in relation to motivational baseline scores.

This case study underscores the value of integrating psychometric tools like the AMI into the operational and strategic fabric of a police department. When thoughtfully implemented, motivation assessments can foster not only more effective staffing decisions but also a stronger, more self-aware, and resilient organizational culture. The project served as a model for other agencies exploring the intersection of psychological science, leadership development, and the future of ethical, data-driven law enforcement.

Conclusion

The integration of motivation science into law enforcement is not a luxury—it is a necessity for modern personnel management and organizational excellence. As law enforcement agencies grapple with rising demands for transparency, accountability, and legitimacy, understanding the psychological underpinnings of officer performance becomes imperative. Tools like the Achievement Motivation Inventory (AMI), along with complementary assessments, offer an empirically grounded means of evaluating the internal drivers that shape behavior, resilience, and engagement across various roles and career stages.

When used ethically and strategically, psychometric assessments can revolutionize how agencies recruit, train, develop, and retain personnel. They enable leaders to move beyond superficial performance metrics and uncover deeper insights into what energizes their workforce. For example, an officer with high persistence and a goal-oriented mindset might thrive in long-term investigations, while one with elevated interpersonal sensitivity may excel in community relations. Tailoring assignments, mentorships, and development plans to these profiles fosters greater job satisfaction, reduces burnout, and enhances long-term organizational commitment.

Moreover, motivation assessments empower officers to better understand themselves. Self-awareness is a cornerstone of emotional intelligence and effective leadership, and it begins with identifying what one values, fears, and strives to achieve. By providing officers with structured insights into their motivational profiles, departments can promote not only professional growth but also psychological well-being and ethical self-regulation.

The utility of these tools extends far beyond individual development. From a systems perspective, motivation data can inform the design of leadership pipelines, identify cultural blind spots, and illuminate patterns of disengagement before they manifest as attrition or misconduct. They also support equity by shifting evaluations away from informal, subjective impressions toward structured, validated criteria that recognize diverse forms of excellence. In this sense, motivational assessments help democratize advancement opportunities and reinforce merit-based practices.

Yet their success hinges on thoughtful implementation. Motivation assessments must be introduced with transparency, interpreted with nuance, and integrated into holistic talent strategies. Ethical safeguards—including informed consent, confidentiality, and developmental framing—are essential to ensure that assessments build trust rather than suspicion. Cultural and contextual considerations must also be prioritized, with tools validated against the unique stressors, diversity, and occupational cultures of law enforcement populations.

Looking forward, the role of motivation science in policing is likely to expand. As artificial intelligence, predictive analytics, and performance dashboards become more prevalent, integrating psychometric data will allow for richer, more personalized approaches to personnel management. The question is not whether we can measure motivation, but whether we are prepared to act on what we find—to lead with insight, assign with intention, and cultivate officers who serve not just with compliance, but with purpose.

Measuring what matters begins with understanding what motivates. In that understanding lies the foundation of professional excellence, organizational integrity, and enduring public trust. By investing in the psychological well-being and motivational alignment of their personnel, law enforcement agencies can not only forge safer communities but also stronger, more resilient institutions equipped to meet the demands of 21st-century policing.

Chapter 5: Power, Affiliation, and the Dark Side of Motivation

Introduction

In the realm of law enforcement, motivation is often seen as a source of strength—a driving force behind courage, service, and excellence. Officers regularly face volatile, high-stakes situations that demand emotional regulation, moral clarity, and strategic decision-making. In this context, motivation is not merely an internal driver but a critical operational asset. Yet motivation, like any powerful force, has a dual nature. When channeled through ethical frameworks and professional accountability, it can fuel integrity, leadership, and community trust. When misdirected or left unexamined, it can manifest as misconduct, abuse of authority, and toxic workplace cultures.

The study of motivation in policing is not new, but its importance has grown in an era marked by heightened public scrutiny, complex social dynamics, and an evolving understanding of organizational psychology. While much of the discourse focuses on performance enhancement and officer wellness, it is equally vital to examine the unintended consequences of certain motivational profiles. A desire to lead, belong, or achieve—while seemingly noble—can turn problematic when entangled with insecurity, unchecked power, or institutional complacency.

This chapter draws on David McClelland's Three Needs Theory, which identifies three primary motivational drivers: achievement (nAch), power (nPow), and affiliation (nAff). Each of these needs plays a pivotal role in shaping officer behavior, career trajectories, and leadership approaches. However, when distorted or disproportionately emphasized, they can contribute to organizational dysfunction. For example, the need for power, when unmoored from ethical constraints, may lead to coercive supervision or retaliatory conduct. Similarly, a heightened need for affiliation might foster camaraderie, but it can also support a culture of silence that impedes accountability.

By applying McClelland's framework to the specific realities of law enforcement, this chapter seeks to provide not only diagnostic insight but also practical guidance. How do these motivational needs influence behavior on the street, in roll call rooms, and in leadership offices? How can agencies support officers in developing self-awareness about their drives while cultivating systems that reward ethical expression of those motivations? And most crucially, how can an understanding of the darker side of motivation help prevent corruption, reduce misconduct, and support sustainable reform?

This inquiry is not merely academic. It is essential to the development of credible, resilient, and community-oriented policing models. By examining the darker manifestations of these needs—particularly power and affiliation—we gain deeper insight into how well-intentioned traits can become destructive if left unchecked (McClelland, 1961). In doing so, we also uncover pathways for fostering a law enforcement culture that aligns ambition with service, loyalty with transparency, and leadership with ethical responsibility.

Power: The Double-Edged Sword

The need for power (nPow) in McClelland's theory is characterized by a desire to influence others, control outcomes, and attain status. In policing, this drive can be profoundly beneficial.

Officers with a high nPow often rise to leadership roles, excel in high-stakes decision-making, and command respect in volatile situations. These individuals may demonstrate a strong sense of order, discipline, and institutional loyalty, which are essential for maintaining operational control. In environments where decisiveness, confidence, and authority are paramount, officers motivated by power can serve as stabilizing forces, especially during crises or in units that demand strong command presence.

Socialized power—the form that seeks to influence others for the benefit of the organization or the greater good—is particularly valuable in building collaborative teams and mentoring junior officers. Leaders driven by socialized power tend to be motivated by institutional outcomes rather than personal gain. They are often respected as visionaries who can steer their departments toward reform, innovation, and mission alignment (McClelland & Burnham, 1976).

However, the same motivational drive can also lead to problematic behaviors when distorted by ego, insecurity, or a lack of accountability. McClelland distinguished between socialized power and personalized power, the latter being centered on dominance and self-aggrandizement. Personalized power is often characterized by a need to control for the sake of validation rather than service. In law enforcement, this distinction is critical because the organizational structure inherently grants authority to officers—making it easy for personalized power to masquerade as legitimate command.

Supervisors with personalized power orientations may engage in coercive control, bullying, micromanagement, or retaliatory behaviors. They may prioritize obedience over growth, discourage dissent, and frame any challenge to their authority as insubordination. Instead of fostering development, they may suppress creativity and innovation, creating a stagnant and fear-driven workplace culture. This leadership style undermines psychological safety—an essential component of team effectiveness—and fosters organizational silence, where employees hesitate to speak up about concerns or propose new ideas (Detert & Edmondson, 2011).

Consider the case of a precinct commander who consistently bypasses procedural norms to impose unilateral decisions. Subordinates are reprimanded for questioning orders, and promotions are granted not on merit but on compliance. Such dynamics not only erode morale but also increase the risk of unethical conduct as officers mimic or capitulate to authoritarian leadership (Kellerman, 2004). Over time, this style of command can breed resentment, cynicism, and disengagement, particularly among officers whose own values prioritize collaboration and fairness.

The dangers of unregulated power motivation are magnified in settings where oversight mechanisms are weak or selectively enforced. Leaders who operate without checks and balances may come to view themselves as untouchable, leading to a cascade of toxic behaviors ranging from favoritism and nepotism to policy violations and civil rights abuses. This is particularly concerning in high-autonomy assignments, such as narcotics or internal affairs, where visibility is low and discretion is high.

Preventing the misuse of power motivation requires a multifaceted approach. First, departments must prioritize leadership development programs that assess and cultivate emotional intelligence, ethical reasoning, and reflective practice. Second, performance evaluations for supervisors should include upward feedback from subordinates, allowing departments to detect early signs of dysfunction. Third, promotion processes should incorporate assessments of motivational orientation to ensure alignment between leadership roles and personality profiles (Bass & Riggio, 2006).

In sum, the power motive is neither inherently good nor bad. It becomes a double-edged sword depending on how it is developed, expressed, and constrained. When linked to institutional values and ethical leadership, power fuels vision, order, and effective governance. When driven by self-interest or left unchecked, it can distort organizational culture and undermine public trust. Law enforcement agencies must therefore treat power not only as a structural necessity but also as a psychological variable requiring continuous evaluation and ethical stewardship.

Affiliation and Team Dynamics

The need for affiliation (nAff) reflects a desire for harmonious relationships, social belonging, and approval from peers. In law enforcement, where trust and interdependence are paramount, this need plays a vital role. Unlike many professions, policing requires a constant reliance on one's partners and team members for personal safety, emotional processing, and operational success. Officers regularly face traumatic incidents, such as responding to fatal accidents, domestic violence, and armed confrontations. In such contexts, affiliative bonds are not just desirable—they are essential for psychological survival and team cohesion.

Units with strong affiliative cultures often demonstrate high levels of mutual support, informal mentoring, and emotional resilience. Officers in these environments are more likely to seek help, share concerns, and debrief after difficult calls, reducing the long-term impact of stress and burnout. Research indicates that affiliation and perceived social support are strong predictors of reduced psychological distress in law enforcement officers, reinforcing the protective function of team-based solidarity (Violanti et al., 2017; Tuckey & Hayward, 2011).

However, affiliation, like power, possesses a shadow side. When the need for belonging becomes excessive or uncritical, it can override the imperative for integrity, independence, and ethical decision-making. Officers who fear alienation from their peers may engage in groupthink—conforming to prevailing norms or suppressing dissent even when those norms conflict with professional standards. This tendency can foster an insular mindset, where loyalty to the team takes precedence over duty to the public or adherence to lawful procedures.

Loyalty, in this context, can devolve into complicity. Particularly in specialized units, such as narcotics, gang enforcement, or tactical response teams, where personnel often operate with greater autonomy and face higher risks, the development of "us vs. them" mentalities is common. These close-knit groups may create subcultures within the department—complete with their own norms, codes, and informal leadership structures. In such environments, misconduct may be overlooked or even tacitly encouraged if it aligns with group values (Skolnick, 2002).

One prominent example is the "blue wall of silence," a term used to describe the unwritten code among officers not to report on a colleague's errors, misconduct, or crimes. While this code may originate from a desire to protect fellow officers, it often results in a systemic failure to address unethical behavior. Over time, this contributes to a culture of impunity that erodes public trust and damages departmental legitimacy (Westmarland, 2005).

Balancing affiliation with accountability requires intentional and proactive leadership. Supervisors must create environments where connection does not come at the expense of ethical standards. Open dialogue, clear reporting channels, and protection for whistleblowers are critical to ensuring that loyalty to peers does not override accountability to the community and the law. Leaders should reward ethical courage—such as reporting misconduct or challenging harmful norms—while modeling vulnerability and moral integrity in their own behavior (Densten, 2002).

Training programs should also incorporate discussions on ethical tension in group settings. Officers must be equipped with tools to navigate situations where their affiliation needs come into conflict with professional values. Role-play, case studies, and facilitated discussions can help officers recognize and manage these tensions in real time.

Ultimately, affiliation is a double-edged psychological driver. When nurtured ethically, it fosters trust, resilience, and professional solidarity. When left unchecked or manipulated, it becomes a force that shields wrongdoing and stifles reform. Law enforcement leaders must ensure that the affiliative bonds so essential to officer well-being and effectiveness are reinforced by shared ethical commitments—not subverted by misplaced loyalty.

The Dark Side of Motivation

While McClelland's theory was developed to understand and promote positive human motivation, it also reveals how needs can be distorted, magnified, or weaponized in organizational settings. Achievement, power, and affiliation are not inherently virtuous or destructive—they become so based on the context in which they are activated, the maturity of the individual expressing them, and the presence or absence of ethical constraints. When these needs evolve into compulsions—driven by insecurity, narcissism, or a desire for control—the result is often toxic leadership, harmful team dynamics, and systemic dysfunction.

Toxic leaders may initially present as charismatic, competent, or results-oriented. They often rise quickly through the ranks, particularly in hierarchical systems such as law enforcement, where assertiveness and decisiveness are highly valued. However, beneath this exterior often lies a fragile motivational structure, marked by an excessive need for validation (distorted achievement), dominance (personalized power), or acceptance (conditional affiliation). When left unexamined, these needs can overshadow the mission of public service and undermine the psychological safety of those they lead.

Narcissistic tendencies may manifest in self-promotion, hypersensitivity to criticism, micromanagement, and the exploitation of subordinates for personal gain or advancement. Such leaders often struggle to share credit, acknowledge mistakes, or invest in the development of others. Their leadership style becomes more about image preservation than impact creation. Lipman-Blumen (2005) argues that toxic leaders maintain power not by competence, but by manipulating followers through fear, dependency, or misplaced loyalty. This is particularly dangerous in law enforcement, where positional authority is often equated with legitimacy and where hierarchical loyalty can stifle dissent.

Authoritarian leaders, on the other hand, may conflate control with competence. They view dissent as disloyalty, suppress innovation that threatens the status quo, and impose rigid hierarchies that prioritize obedience over creativity. This form of leadership may offer short-term gains in order or compliance but ultimately undermines long-term adaptability and officer morale. These patterns are not merely personality quirks—they are maladaptive expressions of basic motivational needs left unregulated by ethical reflection and organizational oversight.

Transformational leadership—defined by Bass and Riggio (2006) as a style marked by empathy, vision, integrity, and individualized consideration—requires a different kind of motivational maturity. Leaders must develop an awareness of their own internal drivers and actively manage them in alignment with the collective good. They must learn to derive satisfaction not only from personal success but from the success and growth of others. In this way, McClelland's theory is not just diagnostic—it becomes a roadmap for the development of ethical and sustainable leadership.

Recognizing the signs of dysfunctional motivation is critical for early intervention. Common indicators include frequent interpersonal conflict, resistance to feedback, defensiveness, favoritism, emotional volatility, and ethical blind spots. Leaders displaying these symptoms may dominate conversations, silence dissenters, reward loyalty over merit, or make decisions based on personal preference rather than policy or principle. When these patterns emerge, they should prompt both organizational scrutiny and developmental intervention—not only to prevent harm, but to redirect the underlying motivational energies toward constructive expression.

Developmental strategies may include reflective coaching, emotional intelligence training, values-based workshops, and peer feedback mechanisms. These tools help leaders understand how their unmet psychological needs may be distorting their behaviors and provide them with healthier ways of achieving fulfillment. Importantly, such efforts must be coupled with structural accountability, ensuring that the environment reinforces ethical leadership rather than enabling its toxic counterpart.

In sum, motivation is not always noble or neutral. It can become a force for dysfunction when driven by unexamined needs or exercised without boundaries. Law enforcement agencies must therefore treat motivation not as a static trait but as a dynamic force—one that requires continuous cultivation, ethical grounding, and developmental support. By illuminating the dark side of motivation, departments can better identify risk, support leadership growth, and build cultures that prioritize service over self.

Internal Affairs and Ethical Oversight

The application of McClelland's framework is particularly useful in internal affairs investigations and ethics review boards. By understanding the motivational underpinnings of misconduct, investigators can move beyond surface-level infractions to uncover the systemic and psychological drivers that contribute to unethical behavior. Rather than treating violations as isolated acts of poor judgment, departments can approach misconduct as the manifestation of deeper motivational misalignments, often exacerbated by cultural, supervisory, or structural factors.

For example, an officer repeatedly accused of excessive force may not simply be "aggressive" in temperament. Instead, the behavior may reflect a high need for personalized power—an urge to dominate, control, and assert superiority in situations where de-escalation would be more appropriate. These officers may feel most validated when their authority is unchallenged, and they may perceive any resistance as a threat to their status. On the other hand, an officer who conceals a colleague's misconduct may not lack ethical understanding but may be acting from a heightened need for affiliation. The desire to preserve group loyalty, maintain acceptance, or avoid ostracism can override internal moral compasses, particularly in units where silence is normalized and whistleblowing is stigmatized.

These motivational insights should inform not only investigative findings but also the design of remedial actions. While accountability is non-negotiable, departments should consider the benefits of a rehabilitative rather than solely punitive model. Strategies such as motivational coaching, reflective supervision, and psychological counseling can help redirect maladaptive behaviors by addressing the unmet psychological needs behind them. Officers with strong dominance needs may benefit from leadership development programs that emphasize servant leadership and emotional intelligence, while those with strong affiliative tendencies may need structured environments that encourage ethical dissent and provide support for values-based decision-making.

Reassignment to roles better suited to an individual's motivational profile is another underutilized strategy. For instance, a high-achievement officer who struggles in a reactive patrol setting may thrive in investigative work or task force assignments that offer long-term challenges and autonomy. Likewise, an officer whose affiliation needs drive them to prioritize team harmony above all else may excel in community engagement roles, where their interpersonal strengths can be leveraged in ways that align with ethical expectations. Peer mentorship programs can also serve as platforms for healthy modeling, offering guidance from experienced officers who have learned to channel their motivations constructively.

Furthermore, ethics training should move beyond policy recitation to incorporate discussions on motivational risk factors. Officers must be equipped with the self-awareness to recognize how their own needs for power, affiliation, or achievement may influence their decisions, particularly under stress or in morally ambiguous situations. Scenario-based training, reflective journaling, and facilitated peer discussions can be used to surface these internal dynamics and promote adaptive coping strategies.

Supervisors, too, must be trained to identify motivational red flags early. These may include excessive competitiveness, fear of losing status, rigid conformity, or withdrawal from feedback. Leaders who understand the psychological dimensions of misconduct are better positioned to intervene proactively, creating a culture where early correction is possible and where officers feel supported in their growth, not just punished for their errors.

Incorporating McClelland's framework into internal affairs protocols also supports a more nuanced and holistic view of professional development. Rather than casting misconduct in purely moral terms, this approach frames it as a mismatch between internal drives and role expectations—one that can be corrected through ethical guidance, organizational alignment, and motivational recalibration. In this way, ethical oversight becomes not only a mechanism of control but also a pathway to transformation and resilience within the profession.

Conclusion

Motivation is not inherently good or bad—it is a source of human energy that must be understood, guided, and supported within ethical frameworks. In law enforcement, where power, affiliation, and stress converge in high-stakes environments, the potential for motivational forces to either uplift or derail professional conduct is profound. McClelland's Three Needs Theory provides a powerful lens for making sense of these dynamics, offering insight into why some officers rise as transformational leaders while others falter under the weight of unexamined psychological drives.

The stakes of misaligned motivation in policing are uniquely high. Officers wield significant discretionary power, often operate with limited supervision, and make decisions that affect lives, liberties, and community trust. When these decisions are fueled by unchecked desires for dominance, validation, or group approval, the result can be toxic cultures, abuses of power, and institutional breakdown. Conversely, when motivation is ethically aligned—when officers are driven by a desire to serve, to grow, and to protect—policing becomes a noble profession capable of restoring hope and justice.

Agencies that invest in understanding these motivational dynamics are better equipped to develop ethical leaders, maintain team integrity, and promote cultures of accountability. This requires a shift from a narrow focus on behavior correction to a broader emphasis on psychological development and organizational alignment. Leadership training, ethics programs, and supervisory practices must all be retooled to recognize and respond to the underlying motivational patterns that shape officer behavior.

By aligning leadership development with psychological insight, departments can move beyond reactive discipline toward the proactive cultivation of ethical, resilient officers. This involves creating safe spaces for reflection, providing feedback that speaks to internal drivers, and building promotion systems that reward not only performance but also integrity, emotional maturity, and team contribution. The best leaders in policing are not those who seek power for its own sake, but those who understand the responsibility that comes with it and use their influence to elevate others.

Moreover, the alignment of motivation with ethical purpose is not just an internal imperative—it is an external necessity. Communities today demand more than technical proficiency from law enforcement; they seek compassion, fairness, and transparency. Departments that fail to attend to the inner workings of officer motivation risk producing public servants who are disengaged at best and dangerous at worst.

The goal is not to eliminate powerful motivations such as the desire for achievement, connection, or influence. Rather, the challenge is to ensure these motivations are channeled in service of justice, not ego; community, not clique; reform, not repression. When officers are supported in developing a deep understanding of their own psychological drives, they become more self-aware, more ethically grounded, and more effective in their role as stewards of the public trust.

In this alignment—between personal motivation and professional ethics—lies the future of credible, compassionate, and competent policing. It is not enough to train officers in tactics and procedure; we must also cultivate their inner architecture, so that the badge they wear is matched by a mindset prepared to lead, to listen, and to serve with honor.

Chapter 6: Motivation and the Ethical Compass

Introduction

In the evolving landscape of 21st-century policing, the ethical conduct of law enforcement officers is no longer viewed solely through the lens of rules, regulations, or compliance mechanisms. While formal codes of ethics and professional standards remain critical cornerstones of accountability, they are increasingly recognized as insufficient on their own. A growing body of research in behavioral science, occupational psychology, and criminology underscores the need for a more nuanced understanding of the internal forces that shape officer conduct—particularly the role of intrinsic motivation in sustaining ethical behavior over time (Deci & Ryan, 1985; Miller, 2006).

Modern policing now operates under conditions of unprecedented complexity and scrutiny. Officers must navigate not only crime scenes but also the expectations of diverse communities, evolving legal norms, and the persistent gaze of body cameras and public opinion. High-profile incidents of police misconduct—ranging from excessive use of force to corruption and systemic bias—have eroded public confidence in many jurisdictions, prompting calls for reform that go beyond surface-level compliance measures. In this context, it is no longer sufficient to ask whether officers know the rules; the critical question is whether they are internally motivated to live by them—especially in high-stakes, ambiguous, or unsupervised situations (Skolnick & Fyfe, 1993; Punch, 2009).

This chapter explores the intersection of motivation and ethics in law enforcement, arguing that sustained ethical conduct is most reliably rooted in a deeply internalized sense of purpose, identity, and values. Intrinsic motivation—defined by Deci and Ryan (1985) as the drive to act out of interest, meaning, or personal commitment—is essential for officers who must often make split-second decisions with far-reaching moral consequences. When officers are animated by internal values such as justice, compassion, and public service, they are more likely to act ethically even in the absence of external rewards or punitive threats.

We draw upon David McClelland's Three Needs Theory (1961), which identifies achievement, power, and affiliation as core human motivators, and Self-Determination Theory (Deci & Ryan, 2000), which emphasizes autonomy, competence, and relatedness as the foundations of internal motivation. These frameworks provide powerful tools for understanding how different motivational profiles influence officer behavior—and, importantly, how departments can leverage this insight to support ethical resilience. For example, officers with high achievement motivation (nAch) may be especially committed to moral excellence as part of professional identity, while those with high need for power (nPow) or affiliation (nAff) may face unique temptations or blind spots if those needs are unmet or misdirected (McClelland & Burnham, 1976; Densten, 2002).

Understanding the motivations that shape ethical behavior is not an abstract academic concern—it is a practical imperative for leadership, policy, and public trust. Agencies that proactively nurture intrinsic motivation through mission clarity, mentorship, role modeling, and values-based training are more likely to develop officers who self-regulate, admit mistakes, and hold themselves accountable. Conversely, when motivational needs are ignored—or when organizational cultures overemphasize control, competition, or punishment—ethical behavior may become conditional, performative, or unsustainable (Kaptein, 2011).

As the profession continues to grapple with calls for reform and transformation, the time has come to re-center motivation in conversations about ethics and leadership. Cultivating ethical behavior requires more than procedural knowledge—it requires psychological insight, organizational alignment, and a commitment to developing officers who are not only rule followers, but moral agents. By embedding motivational awareness into recruitment, training, supervision, and institutional values, law enforcement can move toward a model of accountability that is not merely reactive, but proactive—anchored not just in oversight, but in purpose, identity, and the public good.

The Role of Intrinsic Motivation in Ethical Behavior

Intrinsic motivation—defined as the internal desire to perform actions for their own sake, rooted in interest, meaning, or values (Deci & Ryan, 1985)—is a cornerstone of ethical resilience. In the context of policing, this type of motivation is particularly important because of the high degree of discretion officers must exercise in the field. Unlike many other professions, officers frequently encounter situations where they must make rapid ethical judgments without immediate supervision or clear precedents. In such moments, the strength of their internal moral compass becomes the most critical determinant of behavior.

Officers who are intrinsically motivated are more likely to engage in ethical decision-making because their sense of right and wrong is anchored in deeply held values rather than fear of punishment or hope for reward. Values such as fairness, justice, service to the community, empathy, and respect for human dignity serve as internal guides that shape behavior even under pressure. These values become especially salient in moments of ambiguity, such as handling mentally ill individuals in crisis, managing use-of-force decisions, interacting with vulnerable populations, or intervening when a colleague crosses ethical lines.

McClelland's need for achievement (nAch) aligns with this perspective (McClelland, 1961), as high-achievement officers often strive to meet personal standards of excellence, which can include moral excellence. Officers with high nAch are not satisfied with merely following procedures; they seek to excel in their performance and often view ethical conduct as a core component of their professional identity. For these officers, doing the right thing is not a box to check—it is a source of pride and professional fulfillment. This self-driven pursuit of excellence acts as a buffer against ethical lapses, especially in environments where external oversight is weak, inconsistent, or perceived as unfair.

Moreover, research has shown that intrinsic motivation is associated with greater psychological well-being, job satisfaction, and resilience (Ryan & Deci, 2000). These qualities are essential in a profession marked by trauma, scrutiny, and operational complexity. Officers who are internally motivated are better equipped to manage the emotional toll of policing, sustain ethical behavior over time, and bounce back from challenges without becoming cynical or disengaged. They are more likely to experience a sense of purpose in their work, which strengthens their commitment to both ethical ideals and public service.

Importantly, fostering intrinsic motivation requires supportive organizational environments. Departments that emphasize ethical leadership, recognize and celebrate ethical behavior, promote transparency, and allow for autonomy in decision-making create conditions where intrinsic motivation can flourish. Training programs that incorporate moral reasoning, community engagement, and reflective practices further reinforce this motivation. Conversely, cultures that rely solely on punishment, micromanagement, or rigid hierarchies may inadvertently suppress internal moral drives, fostering environments of fear, disengagement, or moral indifference.

Intrinsic motivation also facilitates peer influence in a positive direction. Officers who are intrinsically motivated often serve as role models for others, creating a ripple effect that elevates the ethical tone of the entire agency. They may be more likely to mentor new recruits, challenge unethical practices, or support colleagues who are grappling with moral dilemmas. This type of informal leadership reinforces ethical standards in ways that formal policies alone cannot achieve.

In summary, intrinsic motivation provides the psychological infrastructure that enables officers to act with integrity even in the most challenging circumstances. It transforms ethics from a compliance requirement into a personal mission, making ethical behavior sustainable, authentic, and meaningful. By cultivating this internal drive, law enforcement agencies can build a workforce that upholds public trust not because it is mandated, but because it is deeply valued and personally fulfilling.

Motivation as a Foundation for Accountability

Accountability in law enforcement is not merely about oversight mechanisms—it is also about self-regulation. While policies, internal affairs units, and civilian review boards serve important roles in identifying and addressing misconduct, they are ultimately reactive in nature. The most sustainable form of accountability arises when officers internalize ethical standards and are motivated to adhere to them without external compulsion.

Officers who possess a strong intrinsic motivation for ethical behavior are more likely to engage in self-monitoring, admit mistakes, and accept responsibility for their actions. This self-regulatory capacity is essential in a profession where split-second decisions can have life-altering consequences. Motivation becomes the engine behind personal integrity, influencing whether an officer views accountability as a burden or a duty. Officers who are intrinsically motivated to uphold justice do not see accountability as a threat, but rather as a reaffirmation of their professional identity.

Self-regulation also fosters a learning-oriented culture. Motivated officers are more likely to seek feedback, engage in reflection, and use past experiences as learning opportunities. They are open to constructive criticism and see accountability mechanisms not as punitive but as developmental. This mindset is critical in creating a growth-oriented department where ethical and professional development are ongoing priorities.

Furthermore, departments that cultivate environments that support autonomy, competence, and ethical alignment—as described in Deci and Ryan's Self-Determination Theory—are more likely to foster motivated officers who uphold professional standards even in challenging environments. Autonomy-supportive leadership, ethical role modeling, and meaningful feedback are essential components of this motivational ecosystem (Deci & Ryan, 2000). Supervisors who respect officer autonomy and provide opportunities for meaningful contribution foster a sense of ownership and responsibility, which in turn enhances ethical accountability.

In contrast, environments that emphasize rigid compliance, micromanagement, or fear-based discipline may inadvertently suppress intrinsic motivation. Officers in such environments may appear to conform outwardly while disengaging internally, leading to ethical blind spots and a decline in morale. Effective accountability systems, therefore, must be grounded in a holistic understanding of motivation that blends structural oversight with psychological empowerment.

In sum, motivation provides the internal scaffolding upon which external accountability measures can rest. By nurturing intrinsic motivation within officers and creating supportive institutional cultures, law enforcement agencies can move toward a model of accountability that is both ethical and enduring.

When Motivation Fails: Pathways to Misconduct

Ethical lapses in law enforcement frequently stem not from ignorance of rules, but from failures in motivational alignment. When the internal psychological drivers that support ethical behavior become distorted or misaligned with organizational values, officers may begin to act in ways that are incongruent with professional standards. These failures are often rooted in an overreliance on extrinsic motivators—such as promotions, fear of punishment, peer approval, or status—which can render ethical conduct conditional, situational, and fragile.

Officers who operate primarily on extrinsic motivators are more likely to engage in misconduct when those external rewards change or become inaccessible. For instance, an officer motivated by public recognition may take shortcuts or manipulate data to appear successful, while one driven by fear of discipline may hide mistakes rather than report them. In both cases, ethical behavior becomes transactional rather than a reflection of internal values or a commitment to justice.

McClelland's theory offers important insights into how specific psychological needs—particularly the need for power (nPow) and affiliation (nAff)—can become maladaptive when left unchecked. The need for power, while useful for leadership and assertiveness, can devolve into coercion, authoritarianism, and abuse of authority when it takes on a personalized rather than socialized form (McClelland & Burnham, 1976). Officers high in personalized power motivation may equate dominance with competence, leading to behaviors such as intimidation, retaliation, or excessive use of force. These behaviors often escalate in the absence of ethical feedback, supervisory intervention, or peer accountability.

Similarly, the need for affiliation, which is typically associated with loyalty and teamwork, can foster ethical blind spots when it becomes excessive. Officers with high nAff may avoid reporting misconduct to protect peer relationships, rationalize unethical actions to preserve group cohesion, or become complicit through silence. This dynamic contributes to the persistence of groupthink and the so-called "blue wall of silence," wherein the preservation of in-group loyalty undermines transparency and accountability (Skolnick, 2002). The resulting culture often marginalizes officers who speak out, eroding moral courage and discouraging critical reflection.

These motivational distortions are not merely individual shortcomings—they are also symptomatic of broader organizational failures to foster ethical environments. Over time, they can normalize misconduct, marginalize ethical voices, and create toxic work environments where unethical behavior is overlooked, tolerated, or even rewarded. In such contexts, officers may perceive that conformity is more valuable than integrity, and that silence is safer than standing up for what is right.

Understanding the motivational roots of misconduct enables departments to move beyond symptom-level interventions and address the underlying psychological drivers that contribute to ethical erosion. This requires more than punitive measures or reactive policy reforms. To counteract these risks, agencies must adopt motivationally informed approaches to ethics training, supervision, recruitment, and disciplinary processes.

This includes creating structured spaces where officers can reflect on their personal drivers, receive feedback on how those drivers manifest in behavior, and build strategies for aligning motivation with professional values. Developmental initiatives, such as motivational coaching, scenario-based training with ethical complexity, and peer-led ethical discussions, can shift the ethical conversation from one focused on compliance to one rooted in authentic character development and moral commitment.

Ultimately, addressing motivation failures is not only about correcting behavior—it is about cultivating the kind of ethical resilience and moral agency that empowers officers to act with integrity under pressure. In doing so, law enforcement agencies reinforce a culture where ethics is not just expected, but internally embraced and externally exemplified.

Building Ethical Resilience in High-Risk Environments

Ethical resilience refers to the capacity to maintain moral conduct in the face of adversity, temptation, or institutional dysfunction (Rest & Narvaez, 1994; Kaptein, 2011). In law enforcement, this resilience is essential for officers who routinely operate in volatile, ambiguous, and high-stakes environments. It is one thing to act ethically under ideal conditions—it is another to do so when facing peer pressure, organizational failure, or personal stress.

Developing ethical resilience requires more than compliance training or memorizing codes of conduct. It involves cultivating an internal motivational framework that reinforces ethical identity, promotes critical self-reflection, and supports long-term professional purpose. Officers must learn not only what is right but also how to stay grounded in their values when external pressures make ethical action difficult.

Agencies can strengthen ethical resilience by integrating motivational insights into every level of training, supervision, and policy development. Key strategies include:

- Embedding moral reasoning and values-based decision-making into tactical and operational training. Officers should be equipped not only with technical skills but also with ethical reasoning frameworks that help them assess the broader impact of their actions.

- Encouraging officers to reflect on their motivations and the ethical triggers that prompt them. Regular opportunities for structured reflection, journaling, or discussion groups can help officers remain aware of how their internal drivers influence behavior.

- Offering mentorship programs that model ethical leadership and internal accountability. Pairing newer officers with respected mentors helps socialize them into a culture of integrity while providing a support system for navigating ethical challenges.

- Creating feedback systems that recognize ethical courage, not just performance outcomes. By publicly valuing actions that demonstrate ethical fortitude—such as whistleblowing, de-escalation, or admitting errors—departments can normalize and reinforce ethical behavior.

- Establishing wellness and peer support programs that address the psychological toll of ethical dilemmas and provide officers with non-punitive spaces to process experiences. Ethical resilience is not just a rational capacity—it is also emotional and psychological, and must be nurtured as such.

- Integrating motivational assessment tools into recruitment, evaluations, and promotions. Understanding what motivates officers enables leadership to identify individuals at risk for ethical drift and provide targeted development or intervention.

Ethical resilience is both an individual trait and a systemic outcome. It emerges not only from an officer's character but also from the organizational context that shapes their choices. Departments must therefore model ethical behavior at every level of leadership, articulate clear values, and ensure that ethical actions are supported, protected, and rewarded.

Ultimately, ethical resilience represents a proactive approach to integrity in policing. It positions officers not as passive rule-followers but as moral agents capable of navigating complex realities with clarity, conviction, and compassion. In doing so, it builds a profession that is both principled and prepared.

Conclusion

The ethical compass of a law enforcement officer is not calibrated by policy alone—it is shaped by a confluence of psychological, social, and organizational forces. Among these, motivation stands out as both a predictor and protector of ethical conduct. Intrinsic motivation—rooted in personal values such as justice, fairness, and service—serves as a critical buffer against misconduct and a foundation for sustaining public trust. Officers who possess a strong internal ethical framework are less reliant on external controls and more resilient in the face of situational pressures, moral dilemmas, or peer influences.

When officers are empowered to align their internal values with their professional duties, they are more likely to act with integrity, courage, and transparency. This alignment fosters ethical behavior that persists even under conditions of stress, ambiguity, or institutional dysfunction. It enables officers to maintain a consistent moral stance regardless of external changes in leadership, policy, or public opinion. Intrinsic motivation, when nurtured, promotes self-regulation, critical moral reflection, and a sense of moral agency that cannot be legislated into existence.

Departments that recognize and support this intrinsic motivational base through autonomy-supportive leadership, mentorship, ethical feedback systems, and values-based training are investing in long-term cultural resilience. These interventions do not simply enforce compliance—they inspire commitment and moral investment in the profession. Officers who feel personally invested in the ethical mission of policing are more likely to go beyond procedural minimums and embody values such as empathy, accountability, and service-minded leadership. They become role models, not because they are told to be, but because their internal compass naturally points in that direction.

In this context, ethical policing becomes a collective endeavor supported by institutional design and cultural reinforcement. Departments that institutionalize motivational awareness create environments where ethical courage is normalized and rewarded. These agencies are better equipped to detect early warning signs of misconduct, foster restorative approaches to error, and prevent the erosion of morale and public legitimacy that accompanies repeated ethical failures.

Ultimately, in a profession where the consequences of ethical failure can be devastating—both for communities and for the legitimacy of the institution—understanding and cultivating motivation is not just good practice; it is a moral imperative. Motivation is not a peripheral concept in professional ethics—it is central to it. By embedding psychological insight into recruitment, leadership development, training, supervision, and policy, law enforcement agencies can cultivate a new generation of officers who not only adhere to the rules but also embody the spirit of justice with unwavering purpose. This approach does not simply reduce ethical violations; it redefines what it means to serve with honor in an increasingly complex and scrutinized world.

Chapter 7: Culture as the Crucible of Motivation

Introduction

In the realm of law enforcement, motivational theories—such as McClelland's Three Needs Theory (1961) and Deci and Ryan's Self-Determination Theory (1985)—have long been employed to understand officer behavior, enhance performance, and promote ethical decision-making. These frameworks highlight the intrinsic and extrinsic drivers that influence officers' choices, values, and sense of purpose. However, as compelling and comprehensive as these theories may be, they operate within a broader system that can either amplify or erode their effectiveness: organizational culture.

The enduring truth remains that even the most self-driven, achievement-oriented, or ethically committed officer can be shaped, constrained, or redirected by the culture in which they operate. Organizational culture—defined as the shared values, beliefs, norms, and assumptions that guide behavior within an institution (Schein, 2010)—acts as the context within which all motivation is either nurtured or suppressed. As management theorist Peter Drucker famously asserted, "Culture eats strategy for breakfast," a sentiment that holds especially true for motivation in high-stakes, hierarchical, and often politically scrutinized environments like policing.

Culture shapes not only what is rewarded or punished but what is perceived as normal, desirable, or even possible. Officers may enter the profession with a strong sense of justice and public service, only to find themselves in organizational environments that valorize cynicism, loyalty over integrity, or procedural compliance over critical thinking (Skolnick, 2002). In such climates, internal motivation can be slowly eroded, replaced by learned helplessness, ethical fatigue, or performative behavior that seeks only to avoid punishment or gain status.

Moreover, the distinction between individual disposition and motivational climate becomes critical. While motivation can be conceptualized as a psychological trait within an individual, the motivational climate refers to the collective psychological environment that promotes or inhibits motivation across a group or department (Ames, 1992). This climate is constructed through leadership practices, communication patterns, feedback mechanisms, and informal norms that signal what truly matters within an organization. A department that espouses community trust on paper but rewards arrest quotas and overlooks misconduct, for example, sends a powerful message about what behaviors are genuinely valued.

This chapter explores the interplay between organizational culture and officer motivation, emphasizing the necessity of cultivating environments that sustain resilience, accountability, and purpose. It interrogates how motivational climates differ from individual motivation, how toxic or demoralizing cultures suppress intrinsic drivers, and how leadership can diagnose and transform motivational dysfunction. Case studies, empirical literature, and practical models will be utilized to demonstrate both the risks associated with cultural misalignment and the potential benefits of culture-driven reform.

Ultimately, understanding the influence of culture is not just an academic exercise—it is a leadership imperative. In an era where public trust is fragile, recruitment is strained, and officer wellness is paramount, building motivationally supportive cultures is essential not only for ethical policing but for the long-term legitimacy of the institution itself.

Organizational Culture Defined

Organizational culture encompasses the deep-rooted patterns of behavior, values, and shared assumptions that shape the everyday realities of a workplace. According to Edgar Schein (2010), one of the most influential scholars on organizational culture, it can be understood at three distinct levels: (1) artifacts—visible structures and processes; (2) espoused values—strategies, goals, and philosophies; and (3) basic underlying assumptions—unconscious, taken-for-granted beliefs and values. These layers combine to create an environment that influences how members interpret their roles, engage with others, and make ethical decisions.

In the context of law enforcement, culture manifests not only through mission statements and organizational charts but more powerfully through informal norms—often referred to as the "street code" or "cop culture." These unwritten rules govern everything from how officers handle public interactions to how they treat colleagues, manage mistakes, and respond to misconduct (Reiner, 2010). For instance, while a department may formally champion community policing, an entrenched subculture may simultaneously valorize aggressive tactics and discourage vulnerability or emotional expression. Such contradictions can produce cognitive dissonance and ethical fatigue among rank-and-file officers.

Crucially, organizational culture acts as a filter through which individual motivation is expressed. Officers who enter the profession with a high need for achievement (nAch) or a strong intrinsic desire to serve (Deci & Ryan, 2000) may either have their motivation reinforced or undermined by the cultural climate. A culture that prioritizes fairness, mutual respect, and accountability can elevate motivation and align personal values with institutional goals. In contrast, a culture marked by cynicism, hierarchical favoritism, or a lack of procedural justice can lead to disillusionment, detachment, and eventually burnout (Skogan, 2008).

This dynamic is particularly important in understanding why motivation cannot be treated solely as a matter of personality or recruitment. While individual dispositions play a role, the work environment profoundly shapes whether motivation is sustained, redirected, or extinguished. Densten (2002) argues that leadership behavior is a key conduit through which culture affects motivation, noting that ethical leaders serve as "cultural architects" who can model and reinforce prosocial behaviors. Leaders who ignore cultural toxicity or who reward unethical behaviors—whether explicitly or implicitly—risk creating climates where even well-intentioned officers conform to deviant norms to survive or succeed.

Furthermore, culture influences how motivation is rewarded or punished. An officer who demonstrates initiative and ethical courage may be celebrated in one department and ostracized in another, depending on what the culture values. This means that behaviors rooted in strong motivation are not universally supported unless the surrounding culture affirms them. For instance, a whistleblower may be perceived as principled in a transparent culture but labeled a traitor in a culture that prioritizes loyalty over integrity (Kish-Gephart et al., 2010).

Additionally, organizational culture influences how stress is managed, how innovation is welcomed, and how psychological safety is maintained—all of which impact officer motivation. A punitive culture that stigmatizes error can demoralize officers and suppress learning, while a learning-oriented culture that emphasizes growth and feedback can reinvigorate commitment to the profession. According to Van Ginkel and Van Knippenberg (2008), cultures that encourage diverse viewpoints and critical discussion lead to greater engagement and more ethical decision-making among group members.

Figure A; Illustrates the that interaction between organizational culture and motivation is cyclical: culture shapes behavior, which in turn reinforces or reshapes culture.

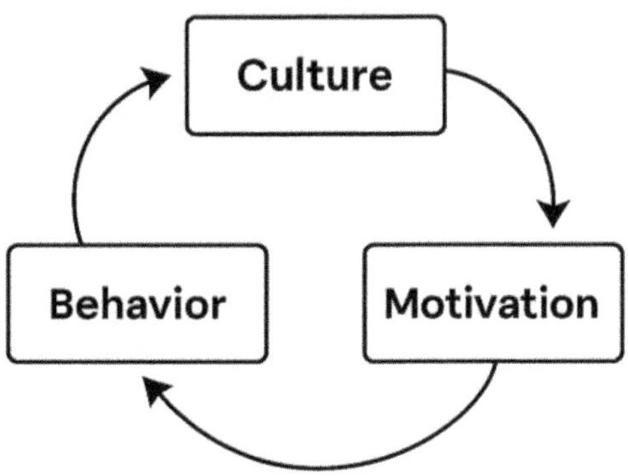

Figure 1. Culture-Motivation-Behavior Feedback Loop

Over time, departments either evolve toward ethical strength and motivational clarity or degrade into dysfunction, where motivation is replaced by compliance or resistance. Thus, leadership must not only focus on individual training or performance metrics but also consistently assess and refine the broader cultural ecosystem in which officers operate.

In summary, organizational culture is not a backdrop—it is an active, dynamic force that shapes the lived experiences of law enforcement professionals. Understanding and shaping this culture is critical to sustaining motivation, ensuring ethical conduct, and promoting wellness in high-stakes policing environments.

Motivational Climate vs. Individual Disposition

While individual disposition—shaped by personal history, psychological needs, and intrinsic values—plays a foundational role in determining an officer's drive, it is the motivational climate that largely determines whether those drives are expressed constructively or stifled altogether. A motivational climate refers to the shared perceptions of policies, practices, and behaviors that signal what is valued, rewarded, and expected within an organization (Ames, 1992). It is a collective psychological environment that can either enhance or inhibit motivation across the department.

McClelland's (1961) Three Needs Theory helps differentiate between individual motivational orientations—achievement (nAch), power (nPow), and affiliation (nAff). However, these orientations do not operate in a vacuum. A high nAch officer, for example, who thrives on setting and attaining challenging goals, may feel empowered in a climate that promotes innovation, recognizes performance, and allows discretion. Conversely, in a culture where initiative is punished or favoritism overrides merit, the same officer may suppress their drive or seek external opportunities, leading to dissatisfaction and eventual attrition (Perry & Wise, 1990)

Officers with a high need for affiliation may similarly experience divergent outcomes depending on the climate. In cultures that emphasize ethical teamwork, psychological safety, and shared mission, these individuals become pillars of cohesion and morale. Yet in environments where the dominant norm is loyalty at any cost, the same affiliative needs may fuel complicity in misconduct or a reluctance to challenge unethical behaviors (Skolnick, 2002). The resulting "code of silence" or "blue wall" phenomenon illustrates how motivational needs can be co-opted by dysfunctional climates.

Moreover, climates that favor extrinsic motivators—such as status, rank, or public accolades—can create zero-sum atmospheres where officers are incentivized to outperform their peers regardless of ethical considerations. In such settings, high nPow officers may exploit hierarchies to exert dominance, while those motivated by achievement might manipulate performance indicators to gain recognition, thereby undermining transparency and accountability (Deci & Ryan, 2000; Van den Broeck et al., 2016).

Motivational climates also shape how failure and feedback are perceived. In growth-oriented climates that encourage learning from mistakes, officers feel empowered to take ethical risks, admit errors, and seek continuous improvement. However, in punitive climates where errors are met with ridicule or formal discipline, even intrinsically motivated officers may disengage or adopt defensive behaviors to avoid scrutiny. As Bandura (1991) noted, self-efficacy and motivation are deeply influenced by the response of one's social environment.

Importantly, climates are not static. They evolve in response to leadership actions, organizational change, and external pressures.

Leaders play a pivotal role in shaping motivational climates by modeling behavior, setting norms, and signaling what is truly valued beyond written policy (Brown & Treviño, 2006). A commander who consistently praises ethical decisions, encourages autonomy, and supports professional development fosters a vastly different motivational climate than one who rules through fear, favoritism, or transactional reward systems.

Understanding the interaction between motivational climate and individual disposition offers law enforcement leaders a powerful diagnostic tool. When morale is low or misconduct emerges, it is insufficient to attribute the problem to "bad apples." Instead, departments should evaluate whether the climate suppresses intrinsic motivation, rewards conformity over courage, or fails to recognize behaviors aligned with public service values.

Figure B; The Motivational Climate Interaction Model depicts the interaction of Individual Disposition (McClelland's needs), Organizational Culture (values, norms), and Motivational Climate (perceived environment), with "Ethical Performance" at the intersection.

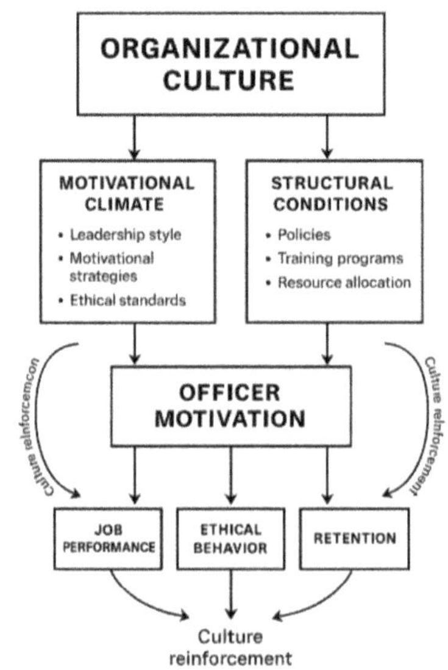

In essence, motivational climate serves as the invisible hand that guides how officers translate internal motivation into external behavior. Departments that fail to cultivate climates conducive to ethical, autonomous, and achievement-driven conduct risk undermining their most dedicated officers and fueling disengagement across the force.

Cultures That Nurture Motivation

Organizational cultures that effectively nurture motivation are intentional in their design, deeply ethical in their leadership, and focused on human development rather than bureaucratic control. These environments do not merely seek compliance; they inspire officers to engage meaningfully with their roles, uphold high ethical standards, and develop a deep sense of professional identity. Several key characteristics define such motivationally supportive cultures:

- Ethical Leadership: At the core of a motivation-enhancing culture is ethical leadership. Ethical leaders are those who model integrity, fairness, and consistency, setting the tone for expected behavior within the organization (Brown & Treviño, 2006). These leaders not only follow rules themselves but also visibly reward acts of moral courage—such as whistleblowing, de-escalation, or community-centered problem-solving. They avoid sending mixed messages about "results at any cost" and instead promote a culture where how success is achieved matters as much as the outcomes themselves. Ethical leadership also includes accountability; leaders must hold themselves to the same standards expected of their subordinates, creating an environment of trust and legitimacy.

- Autonomy Support: Drawing on Self-Determination Theory (Deci & Ryan, 2000), cultures that support autonomy grant officers meaningful discretion in their decision-making, encourage input into organizational decisions, and resist micromanagement. Autonomy fosters a sense of ownership and accountability. Officers in these environments feel that their voices matter, their judgment is trusted, and their work aligns with a higher mission. Research in policing has shown that autonomy is positively associated with job satisfaction, intrinsic motivation, and ethical decision-making (Gillet et al., 2013). When officers are empowered to think critically and innovate, rather than simply execute commands, motivation deepens and professionalism flourishes.

- Recognition Systems: In motivationally rich cultures, performance is not reduced to arrest statistics or citation quotas. Instead, recognition systems reflect a multidimensional view of success. Officers are acknowledged for community engagement, teamwork, mentorship, de-escalation, and ethical decision-making—not just their enforcement output. Feedback is both formal (via evaluations and promotion systems) and informal (via peer recognition and leadership acknowledgment), creating a holistic appreciation of an officer's contributions. This not only sustains motivation but also broadens the definition of what it means to be an excellent police officer.

- Psychological Safety: Coined by Amy Edmondson (1999), psychological safety refers to an environment in which individuals feel secure enough to speak up, share concerns, admit mistakes, and ask questions without fear of humiliation or retribution. In policing, psychological safety is crucial for learning and moral courage. Officers in psychologically safe departments are more likely to report misconduct, seek support after traumatic events, or offer constructive criticism. This open culture promotes transparency, trust, and continual improvement, all of which fuel sustained motivation and ethical performance. Moreover, psychological safety fosters resilience—officers feel more supported, less isolated, and more confident in navigating high-stress or morally complex situations.

Together, these four elements create a synergistic motivational climate. Officers in such departments are more likely to engage in self-regulation, develop habits of ethical reflection, and express long-term commitment to both their agency and the communities they serve. They do not act out of fear or compulsion, but rather from alignment with their internal values and a shared professional purpose.

Importantly, these cultures do not emerge spontaneously. They require deliberate effort, continual assessment, and courageous leadership. Policies must be aligned with cultural values, and incentives must be carefully calibrated to reinforce—not contradict—the mission of ethical service. For example, promoting officers based on disciplinary avoidance or political alignment rather than competence and ethics undermines every other motivation-supporting initiative.

As Drucker's insight reminds us, even the most robust motivational theories can be rendered irrelevant in a toxic culture. But in a nurturing environment, motivation becomes not only sustainable but transformational—fueling a style of policing rooted in justice, humanity, and long-term public trust.

Cultures That Suppress Motivation

In stark contrast to motivationally supportive environments, some law enforcement cultures actively suppress motivation through authoritarian norms, inconsistent values, and systemic dysfunction. These cultures are often characterized by control rather than empowerment, fear rather than trust, and compliance rather than engagement. The impact on officer motivation—and, by extension, on ethical behavior, performance, and wellness—can be profound and corrosive.

Several hallmarks define these detrimental organizational climates:

- Ethical Behavior Is Punished, While Misconduct Is Tolerated: In toxic cultures, officers who act with integrity may find themselves ostracized or penalized, especially when ethical behavior challenges the prevailing norms of silence or complicity. For instance, whistleblowers may be blacklisted, denied advancement opportunities, or subjected to retaliation from peers and supervisors. Simultaneously, officers who bend or break the rules—if aligned with powerful internal cliques—may be protected, praised, or promoted. This inversion of values creates a demoralizing double standard in which moral courage becomes a liability. Over time, officers learn that doing the right thing offers little institutional reward and may, in fact, carry significant risk (Kish-Gephart et al., 2010).

- Promotions Are Tied to Loyalty, Not Merit: In these environments, upward mobility is often less about competence, ethics, or leadership potential and more about political alignment with command staff. Officers who challenge norms, express dissent, or deviate from the dominant culture may find themselves stalled or sidelined, regardless of their qualifications and expertise. This system incentivizes conformity over critical thinking and compliance over integrity. The suppression of merit-based recognition erodes the intrinsic motivation of high-achieving officers (nAch) and fosters resentment among those committed to professionalism and reform.

- Communication Is Top-Down, With Little Room for Dissent or Innovation: Authoritarian cultures often enforce rigid hierarchies where decision-making is centralized and information flows one way—from the top down. Officers are expected to follow orders without question, even when those orders conflict with their own moral or professional judgment. This stifles innovation, undermines psychological safety, and prevents officers from voicing concerns or suggesting improvements. Such climates are antithetical to learning, adaptability, and ethical development (Edmondson, 1999). The lack of participative communication also limits opportunities for mentorship, professional growth, and collective problem-solving.

These cultural elements collectively activate fear-based extrinsic motivation, where officers are driven more by the avoidance of punishment or the pursuit of political favor than by genuine commitment to service or justice. In such environments, internal moral compasses may be overridden by survival instincts. Officers may become passive, cynical, or self-serving—behaviors that, while often framed as individual failings, are in fact rational adaptations to a dysfunctional system (Kappeler et al., 1998).

Furthermore, cultures that suppress motivation often exhibit signs of institutional distrust and burnout. Officers disengage from community-oriented initiatives, resist transparency efforts, and emotionally detach from their roles. The "us versus them" mentality becomes internalized not just in community-police relations but within the department itself, where internal politics eclipse organizational mission. Officers may protect themselves through emotional armor, siloed behavior, or a strict "stay in your lane" mindset—further weakening collaboration and mission alignment.

The long-term consequences of such cultures include high turnover, diminished community trust, an increase in misconduct, and a pervasive sense of futility among those seeking reform. These departments may suffer from cultural inertia, where even well-intentioned reforms fail due to deep resistance at the behavioral and belief levels. As Densten (2002) points out, leadership in such environments often reinforces dysfunction either through neglect or active participation in toxic dynamics.

Ultimately, cultures that suppress motivation do more than demoralize individual officers—they undermine the entire purpose of ethical policing. To counteract these effects, agencies must prioritize cultural audits, solicit anonymous feedback, and invest in transformational leadership development aimed at shifting the deeper values and assumptions that govern diagnosing motivational problems within departments.

Diagnosing motivational dysfunction within law enforcement agencies requires a methodical, evidence-based approach that goes beyond anecdotal observations, isolated complaints, or surface-level performance indicators. Motivation operates beneath the behavioral surface, influencing how officers perceive their roles, respond to stress, and interpret organizational expectations. Therefore, a systematic diagnosis must involve both qualitative and quantitative data sources that reveal underlying cultural and psychological dynamics.

Departments should routinely evaluate their motivational climate using a combination of validated tools and structured processes. Among the most effective methods are:

- Employee Surveys: Instruments such as the Work Climate Questionnaire (Baard, Deci, & Ryan, 2004) or the Utrecht Work Engagement Scale (Schaufeli et al., 2002) assess levels of perceived autonomy, competence, relatedness, and engagement. These surveys can be administered anonymously to gauge internal perceptions of fairness, leadership, morale, and opportunity for growth.

- Focus Groups and Listening Sessions: Facilitated conversations with officers across ranks provide context-rich narratives about the organizational environment. These sessions often reveal tensions between policy and practice, perceptions of favoritism, or inconsistencies in leadership behaviors that undermine motivation.

- Exit Interviews and Turnover Analysis: Systematic reviews of why officers leave can uncover motivational deficiencies that are not evident in day-to-day operations. Common themes—such as a lack of recognition, poor leadership, or limited development opportunities—may point to broader cultural issues suppressing motivation.

- Behavioral Indicators and Organizational Metrics: Certain behavioral patterns often signal motivational erosion. Key indicators include:

    - High rates of absenteeism and presenteeism (where officers are physically present but disengaged)

    - Elevated burnout rates, often reflected in sick leave usage and mental health referrals

    - Increased internal affairs investigations, particularly those involving unprofessional conduct or excessive use of force

    - Widespread resistance to training, policy implementation, or reform initiatives

- Declines in proactive policing, such as community engagement or discretionary enforcement

To gain a comprehensive picture, motivational assessments should be integrated with broader organizational culture diagnostics—such as the Denison Organizational Culture Survey or custom audits of leadership behavior, communication norms, and reward structures. This multi-layered approach allows departments to differentiate between individual performance problems and systemic cultural deficiencies that erode motivation at scale.

For example, if officers consistently report low morale, increased burnout, and skepticism toward leadership—even in the absence of disciplinary issues—this may point to a misalignment between espoused values and lived experiences. In such cases, reforms must go beyond punitive or procedural fixes and instead address foundational cultural deficits that sap motivation, such as inequitable promotion systems, lack of transparency, or fear-based supervision.

Departments can also conduct longitudinal motivational tracking, assessing changes over time in key indicators following major interventions—such as leadership transitions, wellness programs, or training reforms. This allows for the evaluation of not only performance outcomes but also shifts in internal morale, cohesion, and engagement.

Ultimately, diagnosing motivational problems is not a one-time event but an ongoing organizational responsibility. By proactively assessing climate, listening to frontline voices, and responding with targeted, culturally informed strategies, departments can foster healthier work environments that sustain motivation, reduce misconduct risk, and strengthen organizational legitimacy.

Case Study: The Reform of Metro Police Department. In 2018, the Metro Police Department (a pseudonym), serving a diverse urban population, faced a crisis of legitimacy following several use-of-force incidents. Internal surveys revealed low morale, high turnover, and widespread perceptions of favoritism. A motivational climate assessment showed suppressed achievement and affiliation motivations, especially among patrol officers.

In response, the department implemented several reforms: - Introduced ethics-based leadership training for supervisors - Created a recognition program for community-oriented policing - Established officer-led task forces to improve engagement and autonomy - Partnered with a local university to conduct longitudinal motivation assessments.

Within two years, the department reported a 30% drop in complaints, a rise in employee satisfaction, and increased retention. Officers noted a stronger connection between their values and their daily duties, reinforcing the idea that culture change can reignite motivation.

Conclusion

Culture is not a passive backdrop—it is the living, breathing context that shapes how motivation is interpreted, expressed, and sustained in every aspect of organizational life. In law enforcement, where officers navigate a landscape of moral ambiguity, public scrutiny, and high-stakes decision-making, the stakes of motivational misalignment are especially acute. A department's culture determines whether motivation is nurtured or suppressed, whether ethical behavior is celebrated or marginalized, and whether officers are empowered to act as public servants or pressured into cynical self-preservation.

While much attention is often given to individual dispositions, policies, and training curricula, these tools cannot fully compensate for the corrosive effects of a toxic or disengaged culture. An officer who enters the field with a strong intrinsic drive to serve can become disillusioned, disengaged, or ethically compromised if placed in an environment where misconduct is normalized, transparency is absent, or psychological safety is lacking. Conversely, even those with moderate initial motivation can rise to exemplary service when they are supported by ethical leadership, clear institutional values, and a climate that honors their humanity and professionalism.

Departments must therefore adopt a holistic approach that treats motivational climate as a strategic priority. This involves more than compliance—it requires a deliberate investment in cultural conditions that elevate, rather than erode, the intrinsic values of service, justice, and accountability. Key interventions include:

- Diagnosing motivational problems through climate surveys, feedback loops, and cultural audits
- Fostering ethical leadership that models integrity and psychological safety
- Aligning institutional goals with officers' needs for autonomy, competence, and relatedness
- Rewarding prosocial behavior, not just metrics-based performance
- Creating space for moral reflection, dialogue, and emotional growth

By making culture the centerpiece of leadership development, policy reform, and organizational learning, agencies can shift from reactive models of discipline and damage control toward proactive models of ethical cultivation and professional excellence. In doing so, they can reimagine the very meaning of public safety—not as the enforcement of order through compliance, but as the pursuit of justice through human-centered, values-driven policing.

In the final analysis, culture is both the container and amplifier of motivation. It determines whether officers survive the job—or thrive in it. And it is within this cultural crucible that the future of ethical policing will be forged.

Chapter 8: Leading for Motivation: Organizational Strategies That Work

Introduction

Effective law enforcement leadership in the 21st century demands more than the ability to issue directives or ensure compliance with policy. Today's leaders are expected to inspire, empower, and sustain performance in environments defined by complexity, public scrutiny, and high-stakes decision-making. In such a climate, leadership is no longer just about control—it is about cultivating the internal motivations that drive officers to not only meet expectations but exceed them with integrity and purpose.

At the heart of this process lies the science of motivation. Specifically, achievement motivation—the drive to excel, overcome challenges, and meet high standards—plays a critical role in officer development, ethical conduct, and operational success. Yet, despite its proven relevance in organizational psychology, achievement motivation remains an underutilized resource in many police departments. Too often, law enforcement leadership strategies are reactive, focusing on discipline and compliance rather than proactive cultivation of motivational climates that support growth, engagement, and resilience.

This chapter draws from David McClelland's Three Needs Theory—achievement, affiliation, and power—and integrates it with contemporary research in motivational psychology to provide actionable insights for law enforcement leadership. McClelland (1961) emphasized that the most effective leaders are not those who rely solely on authority or charisma, but those who understand and leverage the motivational profiles of their team members to build a culture of performance and purpose.

In practical terms, leading for motivation involves more than offering promotions or issuing commands. It includes strategic behaviors such as providing meaningful feedback, recognizing individual and team accomplishments, offering challenging and growth-oriented assignments, and creating environments of psychological safety and autonomy. These leadership practices not only increase job satisfaction and retention but also reduce burnout, promote ethical behavior, and improve overall departmental effectiveness.

Moreover, understanding the distinction between inspiration and incentives is critical. While tangible rewards have their place, research shows that sustainable motivation is most deeply rooted in internal drivers—values, purpose, and the intrinsic satisfaction derived from meaningful work (Deci & Ryan, 2000). Law enforcement leaders who recognize this dynamic are better positioned to align organizational goals with individual aspirations, fostering a sense of shared mission and moral accountability.

In this chapter, we explore the strategic role of leadership in nurturing achievement motivation within law enforcement agencies. Through theoretical grounding, practical tools, and real-world examples, we illustrate how leadership behaviors can shape the motivational climate of a department—and, in doing so, transform it into a culture of ethical excellence, professional mastery, and enduring public trust.

Leadership Behaviors That Enhance Achievement Motivation

Achievement motivation, or nAch as conceptualized by David McClelland (1961), refers to an individual's internal drive to excel, meet personal standards of excellence, and derive satisfaction from task mastery. In law enforcement, officers high in nAch are typically self-directed, goal-oriented, and committed to continual improvement. However, whether this motivation is activated or suppressed often depends on the behaviors and culture fostered by leadership.

Effective law enforcement leaders serve as motivational catalysts, creating conditions that enable achievement-oriented individuals to thrive. Several core leadership behaviors have been shown to enhance achievement motivation:

1. *Set Clear and Challenging Goals*

Achievement-oriented individuals are most engaged when they are presented with moderately difficult tasks—those that require effort and creativity but remain attainable with persistence and skill (McClelland, 1961). Leaders must therefore strike a balance between clarity and challenge. According to Locke and Latham's Goal-Setting Theory (2002), specific and challenging goals are more effective in improving performance than vague or easy objectives. In a law enforcement setting, this could involve defining clear performance metrics for case resolution, tactical proficiency, or community engagement, while ensuring that officers have the necessary resources and support to meet these objectives.

2. *Encourage Autonomy and Mastery*

Drawing from Deci and Ryan's Self-Determination Theory (1985), achievement motivation flourishes when individuals experience autonomy, competence, and relatedness. Leaders who trust officers to make decisions, pursue independent learning, and own their responsibilities foster a sense of mastery. Rather than rigidly dictating tasks, effective supervisors act as facilitators—providing guidance and removing barriers while allowing officers to take initiative. This approach not only increases motivation but enhances professional identity and long-term engagement (Ryan & Deci, 2000).

In contrast, micromanagement undermines both autonomy and competence. When officers feel overly scrutinized or underutilized, motivation declines and initiative erodes. Over time, this can lead to learned helplessness, withdrawal, or even attrition—particularly among high-potential officers who feel constrained by unnecessary oversight (Gagné & Deci, 2005).

3. Model Excellence and Integrity

Leadership by example is a powerful yet often underestimated motivational force. Officers closely observe the behavior, ethics, and problem-solving approaches of their leaders. When supervisors demonstrate professional excellence, emotional intelligence, and ethical consistency, they set a standard that motivates subordinates to strive for greater heights. According to Bass and Riggio's (2006) transformational leadership model, leaders who exhibit idealized influence inspire followers by serving as role models for behavior and purpose.

This modeling effect is especially important in high-risk, high-stress environments such as policing, where split-second decisions and ambiguous situations demand clarity of purpose. A leader's visible commitment to community service, officer wellness, and procedural justice becomes a moral compass that guides both motivation and ethical behavior.

4. Provide Constructive and Developmental Feedback

Feedback is not merely evaluative—it is motivational. Officers with strong achievement drives are not looking for empty praise; they seek information that helps them grow and improve. Effective leaders provide timely, specific, and actionable feedback that reinforces strengths while identifying paths for improvement (London, 2003). This process affirms the individual's effort and aligns performance expectations with personal development.

Additionally, a growth-oriented feedback culture fosters psychological safety, where officers feel comfortable discussing weaknesses without fear of punitive consequences (Edmondson, 1999). Feedback in this context becomes a tool for empowerment and mastery, not judgment. Leaders who use feedback to coach rather than control are more likely to retain motivated, high-performing officers.

5. Celebrate Milestones and Intrinsic Success

Achievement motivation is sustained when individuals feel that their progress is recognized—not only in formal promotions, but also in the milestones of mastery, such as the successful resolution of a case, growth in tactical skill, or development of mentoring capability. Leaders who acknowledge these contributions—whether publicly or privately—send a clear message that excellence matters. Recognition does not need to be material or grandiose; what matters most is that it is meaningful and sincere (Kouzes & Posner, 2017).

In sum, enhancing achievement motivation is not about pushing harder—it is about leading smarter. Law enforcement leaders who cultivate environments of trust, challenge, recognition, and development tap into the intrinsic potential of their personnel. In doing so, they foster not only performance but also purpose—building teams that are resilient, ethical, and committed to the ideals of public service.

The Role of Feedback, Recognition, and Challenge

In law enforcement organizations, achievement motivation is not a fixed trait—it is a dynamic force that can be nurtured, redirected, or diminished based on how leaders manage three core psychological levers: feedback, recognition, and challenge. Together, these elements create a motivational climate where officers feel valued, capable, and inspired to strive for excellence.

Feedback is one of the most powerful tools available to leaders for sustaining achievement motivation. However, its effectiveness hinges on how and when it is delivered. High-performing officers—those driven by a strong need for achievement (nAch)—crave meaningful, specific input that helps them refine their performance and meet high internal standards (McClelland, 1961). They are less responsive to vague praise or punitive critique and more motivated by feedback that:

- Clarifies expectations and links behavior to outcomes.
- Focuses on improvement rather than solely past mistakes.
- Is timely and continuous, allowing for real-time course correction.

In this context, feedback becomes a developmental dialogue rather than a disciplinary tool. Law enforcement leaders who create feedback-rich environments promote a culture of learning, reflection, and accountability (London & Smither, 2002). Moreover, when feedback is respectful and anchored in mutual trust, it increases psychological safety—making officers more receptive to growth and innovation (Edmondson, 1999).

Recognition serves as a motivational amplifier when it affirms not just outcomes but also effort, values, and ethical behavior. While medals, commendations, and formal awards play a role, research shows that authentic, informal recognition often has a more profound and lasting impact on morale (Grant & Gino, 2010).

In law enforcement, simple gestures such as:

- A handwritten note from a supervisor after a difficult case,
- Public acknowledgment during a roll call,
- Peer-nominated shout-outs in team meetings,

can significantly reinforce an officer's sense of purpose and belonging. Recognition, when aligned with intrinsic values such as service, courage, and professionalism, strengthens internal motivation and reinforces organizational loyalty. It also signals to the broader team that leadership notices and values not just high performance, but also meaningful contributions.

Challenge is the third pillar—and perhaps the most underutilized in traditional police leadership. Achievement-oriented individuals are not content with routine—they thrive on opportunities to stretch their skills, solve complex problems, and master new domains. Leaders who provide such opportunities can unlock latent talent and foster deep engagement (Csikszentmihalyi, 1990).

In policing, meaningful challenges may include:

- Leading cross-functional task forces,
- Mentoring junior officers,
- Taking on long-term investigations or community partnerships,
- Participating in pilot programs or innovation labs.

Importantly, challenges must be appropriately calibrated—too easy, and they breed boredom; too difficult, and they produce anxiety or demotivation (Vroom, 1964). The goal is to foster a state of "flow," where officers are fully absorbed in work that is both meaningful and aligned with their professional strengths.

Beyond individual strategies, constructing teams with aligned motivational profiles enhances organizational effectiveness.

High-performing law enforcement teams are not merely a collection of skilled individuals—they are strategically constructed units where the motivational dispositions of team members align with the tasks, environment, and interpersonal dynamics of their roles. This alignment fosters cohesion, efficiency, morale, and ethical resilience. A well-balanced team leverages diverse psychological strengths—achievement (nAch), power (nPow), and affiliation (nAff)—to meet organizational goals while enhancing individual fulfillment.

To build such teams intentionally, leaders must first gain a clear understanding of what motivates each officer. This is where assessment tools become invaluable, offering structured insights into the internal drivers that influence behavior and performance.

Assessment Tools: Understanding What Drives Each Officer

Beyond individual strategies, constructing teams with aligned motivational profiles enhances organizational effectiveness.

- nAch (Need for Achievement): Prefers challenging tasks, seeks measurable success, values autonomy and mastery.
- nPow (Need for Power): Enjoys influencing others, taking charge, and establishing control—can be socialized (positive leadership) or personalized (dominance).
- nAff (Need for Affiliation): Values connection, teamwork, harmony, and social integration.

Administering such assessments during onboarding, promotion processes, or leadership development programs helps agencies make data-informed decisions about training, assignments, and leadership succession planning.

Team Assignments: Matching Roles with Motivational Strengths

Skilled leaders understand that officers are not a one-size-fits-all solution. They recognize that motivation not only influences performance but also shapes how passionately and ethically officers engage with their work. To harness this potential, assignments should be strategically aligned with each officer's motivational profile.

Officers with a strong need for achievement (nAch) are often most effective in investigative units, analytics, tactical planning, or leadership development programs—areas where their drive for excellence, goal orientation, and problem-solving skills can thrive.

Those with a high need for affiliation (nAff) typically shine in roles centered on relationship-building, such as community policing, school resource officer positions, peer support teams, or crisis negotiation. Their strength lies in empathy, collaboration, and the ability to build trust.

Officers driven by a need for power (nPow) may excel in positions that require assertive leadership, such as SWAT, incident command, or training roles—so long as their motivation is socialized, channeling influence toward team development and collective success rather than personal control.

Misalignment between motivational strengths and role demands can have serious consequences. Placing an affiliative officer in an aggressive, high-conflict tactical unit, or assigning an achievement-oriented officer to a monotonous, low-autonomy task, may result in declining motivation, internal conflict, or ethical disengagement.

Team Culture: Creating Synergy Through Shared Values

Beyond assignments, team culture is the glue that binds individual motivations into collective purpose. A strong team culture:

- Encourages collaboration and interdependence, where officers rely on and learn from each other.

- Celebrates diverse strengths without creating hierarchies of value (e.g., valuing community officers as much as tactical operators).

- Reinforces ethical norms, psychological safety, and mutual accountability.

Leaders must be intentional in shaping this culture through daily rituals, feedback systems, team debriefings, peer recognition, and ethical modeling. For example, a sergeant who encourages officers to reflect on the moral impact of a community engagement operation is reinforcing both nAch and nAff motivations in service of shared public values.

Incorporating motivational alignment into team-building also supports long-term retention and development. Officers who feel "seen," appropriately challenged, and culturally supported are more likely to remain engaged, pursue growth opportunities, and contribute positively to team cohesion.

Equally important is understanding the balance between external incentives and internal inspiration.

In law enforcement leadership, the management of motivation is a delicate balancing act between extrinsic and intrinsic drivers. Extrinsic incentives—including promotions, overtime pay, commendations, and specialized assignments—are often the default tools used by supervisors to influence behavior. While effective in the short term, over-reliance on external rewards risks cultivating a transactional mindset where officers become primarily motivated by what they receive, rather than the values they serve.

The Risks of Incentive-Centered Cultures

While extrinsic rewards—such as bonuses, promotions, or commendations—can play a role in motivating performance, an overreliance on them can lead to unintended and deeply corrosive outcomes in law enforcement settings. When organizational cultures prioritize external incentives above intrinsic values, they risk distorting officer behavior, undermining ethical standards, and compromising long-term institutional integrity.

Gaming the system is one of the most common consequences. In environments where numerical outputs (e.g., arrests, citations, or case closures) are emphasized as primary indicators of success, officers may feel pressured to pursue "easy wins" rather than impactful or equitable policing. This can manifest in inflated arrest statistics, selective enforcement in high-yield areas, or superficial stops that satisfy performance quotas but fail to address meaningful community concerns. Such practices not only degrade data integrity but also erode public trust—especially in communities that feel over-policed yet underserved.

Burnout and cynicism represent another profound risk. When officer worth is equated strictly with productivity—such as the number of calls handled, tickets written, or hours worked—individuals may begin to feel dehumanized, reduced to outputs rather than valued as professionals. The emotional labor inherent in police work, including exposure to trauma, conflict, and community needs, is often overlooked in reward systems focused on efficiency. Over time, this imbalance can lead to emotional exhaustion, diminished engagement, and a pervasive sense of futility or resentment. Maslach and Leiter (2016) describe this as a mismatch between worker values and organizational reward structures—a key driver of burnout.

Conditional motivation further weakens organizational cohesion. When officers are driven mainly by rewards rather than internal commitment, their effort becomes contingent on whether those rewards are present, attainable, or perceived as fairly distributed. Inconsistent or politicized incentive systems can foster frustration, distrust, and disengagement. Officers may lose motivation when they feel overlooked for recognition, when reward criteria are unclear, or when rewards are tied to favoritism rather than performance.

Moreover, the misuse of extrinsic motivators can crowd out intrinsic values, a phenomenon well-documented by Deci, Koestner, and Ryan (1999). Their research on the "undermining effect" shows that when external rewards are perceived as controlling—rather than affirming autonomy or competence—they can actually reduce intrinsic motivation. In policing, this might mean that officers who originally entered the profession to serve and protect begin to prioritize personal gain, status, or scorekeeping, thus weakening their moral compass and emotional investment in the job.

Over time, such cultures may produce what Kunda (1992) calls "instrumental conformity"—behavior that appears aligned with organizational goals but lacks authentic engagement or ethical grounding. This creates a brittle workforce vulnerable to ethical lapses, low morale, and retention issues, especially when reward structures are disrupted due to budget cuts, policy changes, or leadership turnover.

To preserve the integrity of law enforcement institutions, agencies must critically assess how their reward systems interact with motivation and culture. Incentives should be used judiciously, transparently, and in a way that supports—not replaces—officers' internal values and sense of purpose.

The Power of Inspirational Leadership

Inspirational leadership, as opposed to transactional or compliance-based management, functions by elevating meaning, identity, and purpose in the workplace. It appeals to the core of an officer's intrinsic motivation—rooted in values such as justice, fairness, service, and personal growth—rather than external rewards or fear of punishment. When officers feel internally connected to the significance of their role, their performance becomes not just a function of obligation but an expression of personal identity. In this context, motivation becomes both deeper and more enduring.

Officers driven by intrinsic motives are demonstrably more likely to persist through adversity, self-regulate their behavior according to ethical standards, and maintain a sustained commitment to public service even in the face of institutional dysfunction or limited recognition. This kind of commitment is particularly critical in law enforcement, where work is often complex, emotionally taxing, and subject to public scrutiny.

Leaders who inspire tend to practice a set of behaviors that speak directly to these deeper motivations:

- Share a compelling vision: Inspirational leaders consistently communicate the "why" behind policing, helping officers see the moral and societal significance of their daily work. Instead of framing assignments in terms of quotas or control, they emphasize contributions to community well-being, public safety, equity, and justice. This form of visionary messaging allows officers to contextualize their efforts within a broader mission, cultivating what Kouzes and Posner (2017) describe as a "shared aspiration." Officers are no longer just doing a job—they are participating in a cause.

- Reinforce moral impact: These leaders regularly underscore the real-world consequences of ethical and unethical behavior. They highlight moments when officers protected vulnerable individuals, resolved conflicts with empathy, or upheld the rights of marginalized citizens. Such reinforcement promotes a strong sense of moral identity, helping officers feel proud of their role in upholding democratic values and serving as a bulwark against injustice. The moral clarity that inspirational leaders provide becomes a source of pride and resilience.

- Validate personal growth: Inspirational leaders go beyond outcome-based rewards to celebrate progress, learning, and mastery. For instance, an officer who becomes proficient in de-escalation techniques, improves cultural competence, or builds trust with at-risk communities should be publicly recognized—not just those with high arrest statistics or case clearance rates. This broader definition of excellence expands what is valued in the agency, reinforcing a growth mindset and inviting all officers to improve in ways that align with public trust and service.

In this context, inspiration functions as a durable and self-reinforcing source of motivation. Because it is aligned with core values and internal beliefs, it does not require constant external incentives to be sustained. Officers who feel inspired are more likely to take initiative, act with integrity, mentor peers, and maintain morale even during times of resource shortages, public criticism, or organizational uncertainty.

Research in organizational psychology supports this approach. Transformational leadership—characterized by the ability to inspire, intellectually stimulate, and consider the individual needs of team members—is associated with higher job satisfaction, lower burnout, and enhanced ethical decision-making (Bass & Riggio, 2006). In high-stakes professions like policing, where stress and moral complexity are inherent, such leadership is not just beneficial—it is essential.

Ultimately, inspiration outperforms coercion and manipulation because it activates internal meaning rather than external compliance. It creates a culture where officers want to do the right thing, not because they fear punishment, but because it resonates with who they are and what they stand for. In such environments, leadership becomes a force for transformation, not just regulation.

Balancing Both Approaches

While the benefits of inspiration are substantial, relying solely on intrinsic motivation without attending to the structure and reinforcement that extrinsic incentives provide can be insufficient—especially in a large, hierarchical organization like a police department. Officers, like all professionals, operate within systems of recognition, reward, and accountability. The challenge for leaders is not to choose between inspiration and incentive, but to skillfully integrate both in a way that reinforces long-term, ethical motivation.

Extrinsic motivators—such as promotions, bonuses, commendations, and public recognition—remain vital tools in a leader's arsenal. However, their effectiveness depends on how they are framed, delivered, and aligned with internal values. When used in isolation or applied inconsistently, extrinsic rewards can backfire, promoting short-term thinking, competitive resentment, or unethical gaming of the system. When thoughtfully connected to deeper organizational values and personal aspirations, however, they can reinforce intrinsic motivation rather than displace it.

For example:

- Use promotions to recognize ethical leadership and emotional intelligence, not just seniority or enforcement productivity. An officer who de-escalates a volatile situation with compassion or mentors new recruits with integrity contributes just as meaningfully as one who clears cases or logs arrests. Rewarding such contributions signals that the agency values how results are achieved—not just that they are achieved.

- Tie commendations to narratives of moral courage, community trust-building, or service under duress. Rather than issuing generic awards for "excellence," agencies can elevate meaningful stories that showcase resilience, fairness, and community impact. Publicly sharing these examples not only motivates the recognized officer but also inspires others through relatable modeling of virtuous conduct.

- Provide performance feedback that connects day-to-day work with the agency's broader mission. For instance, a supervisor might say: "Your consistent work on this domestic violence task force is a key part of our commitment to protecting the vulnerable. You're helping build safer neighborhoods, one case at a time." Such statements link individual contributions to shared values, reinforcing the officer's identity and sense of purpose.

This integrated approach aligns with findings from Deci and Ryan's Self-Determination Theory (2000), which emphasizes the importance of supporting autonomy, competence, and relatedness. External rewards are most effective when they affirm rather than control—when they acknowledge competence, foster connection, and reinforce self-directed goals.

A balanced strategy also includes guardrails to prevent the misuse of incentives. Metrics used to determine bonuses or promotions must be valid, multidimensional, and free from perverse incentives that encourage manipulation. Including peer input, ethical reviews, and community feedback in reward structures can mitigate these risks.

Ultimately, the goal is to create a feedback loop where incentives reinforce inspired behavior, and inspiration gives those rewards deeper meaning. Officers should not act ethically or work hard merely because they are being watched or compensated—but because they feel personally committed to a mission larger than themselves. Leaders who master this balance will cultivate a workforce that is not only efficient and productive but principled, resilient, and truly aligned with the core values of justice and service.

Figure C. The Balancing Intrinsic and Extrinsic Motivation in Law Enforcement Leadership model illustrates how law enforcement leaders can integrate both intrinsic and extrinsic motivators to build sustainable engagement, ethical behavior, and professional growth.

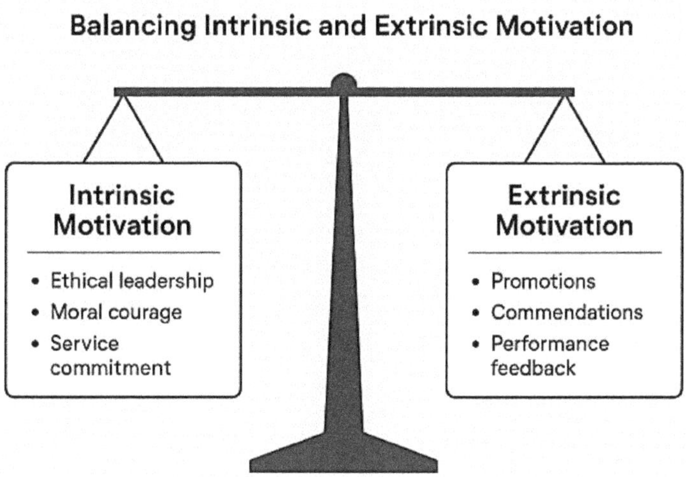

Conclusion

Motivational leadership in law enforcement is not about relying on charisma, issuing commands, or enforcing compliance through rigid control. Rather, it is a sophisticated and intentional approach that draws from psychological science to understand what drives individuals to perform, persevere, and uphold ethical standards under pressure. In this context, effective leadership involves cultivating a motivational ecosystem—one where internal drivers such as purpose, mastery, achievement, and integrity are nurtured and aligned with the goals of public safety and justice.

By integrating McClelland's Achievement Motivation Theory into their leadership practices, law enforcement leaders can go beyond surface-level management to build high-performing, values-driven teams. Officers with high achievement motivation (nAch) thrive in environments where they are challenged, supported, and recognized for ethical excellence and personal growth—not just productivity. Leaders who are attuned to these needs and who tailor feedback, assignments, and opportunities accordingly can elevate both individual and collective performance.

Moreover, in a profession that operates within environments marked by ambiguity, high stakes, and public scrutiny, motivational leadership is essential for sustaining resilience, ethical conduct, and long-term engagement. Traditional top-down leadership models, which rely heavily on hierarchy and external control, often fall short in inspiring the kind of initiative, adaptability, and discretionary judgment that modern policing demands. In contrast, leaders who inspire rather than merely incentivize, who model integrity rather than demand obedience, and who build trust through empathy and fairness are far more likely to earn lasting commitment from their teams.

Crucially, motivational leadership also contributes to a healthier organizational culture, reducing burnout, turnover, and misconduct by fostering an environment where officers feel psychologically safe, professionally valued, and intrinsically motivated. In this way, it serves as a preventive strategy—addressing the root causes of disengagement and ethical lapses before they manifest as crises.

Ultimately, leading for motivation is not an optional add-on to leadership—it is its very foundation. It provides the roadmap for building morally grounded, highly capable, and deeply committed law enforcement professionals who see their role not merely as a job, but as a calling. In the evolving landscape of public safety, where community trust and officer well-being are both under strain, such leadership is not just beneficial—it is an urgent strategic imperative for agencies that seek to thrive, reform, and lead with legitimacy.

Chapter 9: Motivation in Crisis: Resilience, Burnout, and Purpose

Introduction

In the demanding world of law enforcement, motivation is not a static trait but a dynamic force shaped by experience, context, and emotional well-being. Officers enter the profession with a wide range of motivational drivers—such as the desire to serve, the pursuit of justice, or the challenge of solving complex problems—but these motivations are constantly tested by the realities of the job. Daily exposure to suffering, danger, and bureaucratic rigidity, coupled with the pressures of public accountability and internal politics, can wear down even the most intrinsically driven professionals over time.

Unlike many other professions, law enforcement operates in a climate of persistent vigilance. Officers must remain mentally and emotionally prepared to encounter violence, confront life-threatening situations, and witness human suffering—often without the opportunity to fully process or recover from these experiences. This accumulation of psychological strain, known as cumulative trauma (Follette et al., 1994), is compounded by organizational stressors such as inconsistent leadership, unclear expectations, and the stigma surrounding mental health care. As a result, intrinsic motivation—rooted in personal values such as integrity, fairness, and service—can be eroded and replaced by cynicism, detachment, and moral fatigue.

Moreover, the profession's emphasis on stoicism and hyper-resilience can inadvertently discourage officers from acknowledging emotional vulnerability. Over time, unresolved trauma and burnout may distort an officer's sense of purpose, making the job feel like a burden rather than a calling. This transformation has significant implications not only for performance and retention, but also for the ethical and psychological health of entire agencies.

Understanding the intersection between motivation and mental health is crucial for sustaining long-term professional excellence and ethical conduct in policing. Motivation does not exist in isolation—it is intricately linked to an officer's psychological state, sense of identity, and belief in the value of their work. This chapter explores how psychological stress and trauma impact motivational structures, how conditions such as burnout and moral injury (Litz et al., 2009) manifest in policing contexts, and how departments can implement strategies to re-ignite purpose and promote resilience, particularly among veteran officers who may be at higher risk of motivational decline.

By framing motivation as both a psychological and organizational responsibility, this chapter aims to equip leaders, trainers, and mental health professionals with actionable tools to protect, restore, and strengthen the intrinsic drive that fuels principled law enforcement.

The Psychological Cost of Service

Policing is a profession built on repeated exposure to some of the most traumatic and destabilizing events in society—homicides, suicides, child abuse, domestic violence, and the aftermath of accidents or disasters. Each of these encounters leaves an imprint, and over time, the cumulative weight of trauma can have serious psychological consequences. While individual incidents may be absorbed and compartmentalized in the short term, the long-term effects often manifest as post-traumatic stress disorder (PTSD), chronic fatigue, emotional numbing, or moral disorientation.

One particularly insidious form of psychological injury is moral injury, a condition described by Litz et al. (2009) as the emotional suffering that results when an individual perpetrates, witnesses, or fails to prevent actions that transgress their core moral beliefs. Unlike PTSD, which is often triggered by fear-based trauma, moral injury stems from shame, guilt, or a perceived betrayal of ethical standards. In law enforcement, moral injury might arise from being ordered to carry out actions that conflict with one's conscience, witnessing abuses of power, or being unable to help a victim due to policy or resource limitations.

These psychological burdens have a direct and damaging effect on motivational structures. Officers once driven by a deep sense of duty or a passion for justice may begin to experience motivational erosion—a decline in the emotional and cognitive energy available for ethical decision-making and professional engagement. Feelings of futility, moral disillusionment, or emotional exhaustion can prompt withdrawal from colleagues, a tendency toward cynicism toward the public, and a tendency to operate on "autopilot," performing tasks without emotional or ethical investment.

Maslach and Leiter's (2016) model of burnout describes three core components that are highly relevant in policing:

- Emotional exhaustion, which reduces the capacity for empathy and connection.
- Depersonalization, where officers begin to view community members and even colleagues as objects or problems rather than people.

- Reduced personal accomplishment, which diminishes confidence, motivation, and ethical aspiration.

When burnout and moral injury go unaddressed, they not only compromise individual well-being, but also organizational integrity. Demoralized officers may become vulnerable to ethical shortcuts, procedural violations, or even maladaptive coping behaviors such as substance use, aggression, or absenteeism. Moreover, as motivation erodes, the protective factors that sustain moral behavior—such as empathy, professional pride, and a belief in the mission—begin to disappear, thereby increasing the risk of misconduct and public distrust.

The psychological cost of service, then, is not simply a matter of mental health—it is a foundational issue for leadership, accountability, and organizational performance. Agencies that fail to address trauma-related motivational decline risk creating a culture of emotional detachment, low morale, and ethical vulnerability. Proactively supporting officers' psychological and emotional resilience is thus not a luxury—it is a necessary component of professional sustainability and public safety.

Motivational Deterioration and Veteran Officers

While veteran officers are among the most seasoned, tactically skilled, and institutionalized members of a police department, they are also particularly susceptible to a gradual deterioration in motivation. The cumulative effects of prolonged exposure to operational stress, political friction, and organizational stagnation can slowly erode the idealism and drive that many brought with them into the profession. The transition from eager recruit to disillusioned veteran is often subtle and unspoken, manifesting in emotional withdrawal, routine compliance, and a detachment from both mission and meaning.

One key theoretical lens for understanding this decline is David McClelland's Three Needs Theory (1961), which posits that motivation is driven by three fundamental psychological needs: the need for achievement (nAch), the need for affiliation (nAff), and the need for power (nPow). In a policing context, many officers enter the field with high nAch, seeking to make a difference, solve problems, and demonstrate competence. Others may be driven by nPow, motivated to lead, influence, and shape the outcomes of their environments. However, over the years of service, these needs can become unfulfilled, stifled by rigid hierarchies, limited advancement opportunities, political interference, or a perceived lack of impact. The result is not just a flattening of motivation—but a transformation of once-productive needs into apathy, bitterness, or reactive dominance.

Veteran officers, having "seen it all," may cease to seek innovation, growth, or mastery. They may default to minimal effort, reduce discretionary engagement, or become resistant to training and change. Their internal dialogue often shifts from purpose-driven reflection ("How can I serve?") to survival-oriented rationalization ("Why bother?"). This cognitive drift is dangerous not only for their own well-being and ethical decision-making, but also for the younger officers who look to them for cues on how to navigate the profession. When role models become cynics, entire teams can suffer from motivational contagion, where disengagement spreads like a cultural virus.

Re-Igniting Purpose: Organizational and Personal Strategies

Fortunately, motivational decline is not irreversible. The human capacity for renewal—especially when supported by intentional organizational interventions and peer affirmation—is profound. To restore motivation among veteran officers, agencies must adopt a dual-pronged approach that attends both to psychological needs and to the rediscovery of purpose in service. Below are five evidence-informed strategies that departments can implement:

Figure D. This visual model illustrates the progression from motivational decline due to cumulative trauma and institutional strain to pathways for renewal through support, mentorship, reflection, and purpose-driven development.

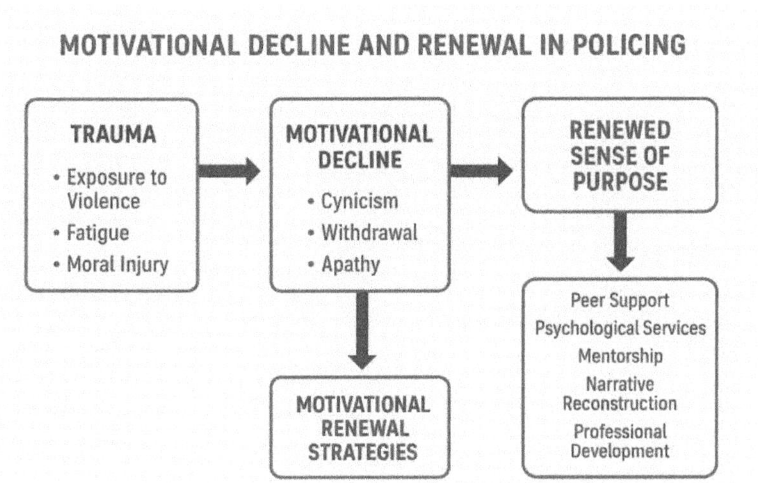

Below are five evidence-informed strategies that departments can implement:

1. *Peer Support Programs*

Peer-to-peer initiatives are among the most effective tools for mitigating emotional isolation and validating lived experience. Officers are often more willing to open up to colleagues who have faced similar challenges than to outsiders. Programs such as peer-led critical incident stress debriefings (CISDs) or scheduled wellness check-ins promote a culture of shared struggle, mutual respect, and healing. Research by Papazoglou and Andersen (2014) has shown that peer support not only improves emotional resilience but also reinforces professional identity, reminding officers that their experiences—though difficult—are not unique or shameful.

2. *Access to Psychological Services*

Stigma-free mental health support is essential in sustaining motivation, particularly for those grappling with moral injury, burnout, or trauma. Departments should ensure confidential access to trauma-informed clinicians, and normalize help-seeking behavior through leadership example and embedded services (e.g., on-site counselors, mental health days, anonymous hotlines). Integrating these services into the culture—not as reactive tools for breakdowns but as proactive tools for resilience—signals to officers that their mental health is both valued and safeguarded.

3. *Mentorship and Purpose Renewal*

Re-engaging veteran officers as mentors to newer recruits can restore a sense of value, responsibility, and professional legacy. Rather than positioning them as outdated or resistant to change, departments can frame them as cultural custodians whose wisdom is essential for institutional continuity and stability. Watching protégés grow and succeed under their guidance can rekindle intrinsic motivation and re-anchor veterans in the "why" of their work. This process transforms cynicism into stewardship and reignites pride in contribution.

4. *Narrative Reconstruction*

As suggested by narrative identity theory (McAdams, 2001), individuals construct meaning through the stories they tell about their lives. Encouraging officers to revisit their careers—to reflect on defining moments, personal growth, and lessons learned—can help reframe past pain as a source of purpose. Structured workshops, journaling exercises, or oral history projects can assist officers in reconnecting to their moral and professional identities. This "narrative therapy" approach also builds psychological coherence, which research has linked to improved well-being and motivation (Adler, 2012).

5. *Professional Development with Meaning*

Offering educational opportunities that go beyond tactical proficiency can invigorate motivation by tapping into officers' deeper values. Topics such as ethical leadership, restorative justice, emotional intelligence, and community engagement provide intellectual and moral stimulation. These programs should be framed not as remedial training, but as professional enrichment, affirming the ongoing development of officers as ethical leaders and civic stewards. When officers are given the opportunity to evolve beyond their operational roles, their sense of self—and, consequently, their sense of mission—can expand accordingly.

Building a Resilient Culture. While individual-level interventions such as therapy, mentorship, and peer support are vital, their effectiveness is significantly magnified when reinforced by an organizational culture that actively promotes resilience. A truly resilient police department does not treat motivation and well-being as secondary or reactive concerns—it weaves them into the very fabric of its leadership, policies, and daily operations. This requires a deliberate shift in mindset: from viewing motivation as a fixed personal trait to understanding it as a renewable and dynamic resource that must be nurtured, particularly in high-stress professions such as law enforcement.

To build this kind of culture, leaders must take proactive steps to normalize the realities of occupational stress and trauma. Conversations about emotional fatigue, moral injury, and psychological strain should not be relegated to crisis moments or whispered in confidence. Instead, they should be integrated into supervisory check-ins, training academies, performance evaluations, and leadership development programs. When leaders model vulnerability and openness about their own challenges, it creates a climate of psychological safety where officers feel empowered to seek help without stigma.

Early recognition of burnout is another hallmark of resilient cultures. Supervisors should be trained to recognize the subtle warning signs—such as irritability, detachment, cynicism, and decreased performance—and intervene constructively. Rather than framing burnout as a personal failure, departments should treat it as a predictable occupational hazard that warrants support and recovery strategies. Instituting regular wellness audits, confidential pulse surveys, and resilience screenings can help identify and address motivational erosion before it becomes institutionalized.

In addition to preventing harm, resilient cultures promote motivation by offering diverse and meaningful career development opportunities. Not every officer is driven by rank or traditional promotion. Some find fulfillment in teaching, mentoring, community engagement, policy reform, or specialized units.

Leaders who recognize and support these varied pathways send a powerful message: that each officer's contribution matters and that growth is multidimensional. This flexibility not only preserves motivation but fosters innovation and loyalty.

Finally, resilient cultures continually reinforce the nobility of public service. Officers must be reminded—through rituals, storytelling, recognition, and institutional messaging—that policing is not merely about enforcement, but about safeguarding human dignity and upholding democratic values. This sense of higher purpose serves as an enduring source of pride, identity, and intrinsic motivation.

By embedding these values into the organizational structure, law enforcement agencies can create environments where motivation is not depleted by hardship, but renewed through support, meaning, and shared mission. A resilient culture doesn't just help officers survive—it enables them to thrive.

Conclusion

Motivation in law enforcement is inextricably linked to psychological health, organizational support, and opportunities for meaningful engagement. It is not a fixed trait but a dynamic process that evolves throughout an officer's career. The cumulative toll of trauma, moral complexity, and institutional strain can erode even the most resilient internal drive. As such, departments must shift from viewing motivation as an individual responsibility to recognizing it as an organizational priority that requires consistent investment and care.

When officers suffer from burnout, moral injury, or chronic disengagement, their diminished motivation not only affects their own well-being but also impacts unit cohesion, community trust, and overall agency effectiveness. This is especially critical for veteran officers, who serve as cultural anchors and informal leaders within their departments. Their attitudes, energy, and sense of purpose can set the tone for entire squads. Re-igniting their motivation is not just a retention strategy—it is a strategic investment in the future leadership and moral compass of the organization.

Comprehensive motivational support includes more than momentary praise or short-term incentives. It demands sustained access to mental health resources, trauma-informed supervision, opportunities for professional growth, and deliberate efforts to reconnect officers with the deeper mission of policing. Through programs like peer support networks, mentorship, reflective practices, and values-based training, agencies can reinforce the belief that the profession is not merely a job, but a meaningful vocation rooted in service, justice, and human dignity.

Ultimately, maintaining motivation across the law enforcement career span is not a luxury—it is a necessity. Departments that prioritize the emotional and motivational health of their officers cultivate not only more ethical and engaged personnel but also more resilient, responsive, and humane policing institutions. In an era where legitimacy and accountability are paramount, rekindling motivation is foundational to both officer wellness and the public good.

Chapter 10: Training for Motivation—From Academy to Promotion

Introduction

In the high-stakes, high-pressure profession of law enforcement, motivation is not merely a passive trait or byproduct of inherent personality. Rather, it is a psychological capacity that can be cultivated, reinforced, and refined over time through intentional training, competent leadership, and an organizational culture that supports internal growth. Officers enter the profession with varying motivational profiles, but the extent to which their motivation endures and evolves depends largely on how agencies train, develop, and support them across the arc of their careers.

Motivation, particularly intrinsic motivation, plays a foundational role in shaping an officer's decision-making, ethical behavior, adaptability, and overall job satisfaction. Yet, traditional police training programs have often focused disproportionately on tactical proficiency, compliance with rules, and rote procedural knowledge, while neglecting the deeper motivational drivers that sustain long-term professional excellence. In failing to explicitly develop achievement motivation, agencies risk producing officers who perform adequately under supervision but falter in autonomy, initiative, and moral reasoning when left to navigate complex and ambiguous field situations.

David McClelland's (1961) theory of human motivation offers a valuable framework for understanding how to train for motivational strength. His concept of the *need for achievement* (nAch) refers to an individual's internal drive to meet personal standards of excellence, solve problems effectively, and succeed in meaningful tasks. Officers high in nAch are not just technically skilled—they are self-directed, growth-oriented, and resilient under pressure. Importantly, research in both educational and organizational psychology demonstrates that achievement motivation can be developed through environmental cues, instructional methods, and reinforcement strategies (Ryan & Deci, 2000; Eccles & Wigfield, 2002).

Effective law enforcement training must therefore do more than transmit knowledge and test procedural compliance—it must intentionally foster motivation. From the earliest stages of recruitment and selection, agencies should evaluate candidates not only for physical and cognitive abilities, but also for motivational potential and value alignment. Academy instruction should prioritize not only tactics but self-efficacy, decision-making under uncertainty, and the psychological skills of reflection, regulation, and perseverance. Field training should provide realistic, challenging, and autonomy-supportive experiences that help officers connect their personal goals to the broader mission of justice and public service.

Moreover, this motivational foundation must be sustained throughout the career trajectory. Promotions should not only reward tenure or task performance but also recognize motivational leadership, mentoring ability, and intrinsic commitment to the profession. Supervisory and command-level training should teach leaders how to cultivate achievement motivation in others by creating climates of psychological safety, purposeful challenge, and ethical accountability (Kuvaas & Dysvik, 2009; Deci, Olafsen, & Ryan, 2017). Motivation must be understood as both an individual trait and a systemic outcome.

This chapter explores how law enforcement training systems—from academy to promotion—can be reimagined to prioritize motivational development as a core educational goal. Drawing on empirical research from educational psychology, motivation science, and contemporary police training literature, we argue that fostering achievement-oriented mindsets is not an optional enhancement—it is a strategic imperative. When motivation is deliberately cultivated, agencies produce officers who are not only technically proficient but ethically grounded, emotionally resilient, and committed to continuous improvement. In a profession where both mistakes and moments of greatness carry immense consequences, training for motivation may be one of the most powerful reforms a department can implement.

Motivational Fit in Recruitment and Selection

Before the first academy lecture is delivered or the first tactical drill is run, one of the most consequential decisions a law enforcement agency makes is who it chooses to hire. The early stages of recruitment and selection shape the motivational architecture of the agency as a whole. If training is to be successful in fostering long-term achievement, commitment, and ethical conduct, it must begin with candidates who possess the psychological predispositions and internal values conducive to public service. Motivation is not a one-size-fits-all construct. As McClelland's (1961) *Three Needs Theory* explains, individuals vary in the relative strength of their needs for achievement (nAch), affiliation (nAff), and power (nPow). A recruit who is high in nAch seeks excellence and thrives on solving complex problems; one high in nAff may be motivated by interpersonal connection and team cohesion; one high in nPow seeks influence, which can be channeled into either positive leadership or authoritarian control depending on the context. When agencies fail to account for these distinctions, they risk hiring candidates who may meet procedural requirements but are misaligned with the ethical and relational demands of modern policing.

Traditional recruitment strategies often emphasize extrinsic rewards, such as salary, job stability, early retirement, or authority. While these aspects are important, they may disproportionately appeal to applicants whose motivation is driven by external incentives (Ryan & Deci, 2000). Research shows that such individuals are more likely to demonstrate compliance-oriented behavior and may be less resilient in the face of ethical ambiguity or professional adversity (Amabile et al., 1994). Intrinsic motivation—grounded in internalized values such as justice, service, and self-improvement—offers a more robust and enduring foundation for ethical policing (Deci & Ryan, 1985). Without attention to motivational orientation, departments risk building forces that may meet immediate manpower needs but lack the deeper drive necessary for sustained integrity and excellence.

To ensure motivational fit, agencies must take a more psychologically informed approach to recruitment and selection. This includes both targeted assessment methods and strategic messaging throughout the recruitment process. Structured behavioral interviews, for instance, can be used to explore past behaviors that serve as indicators of motivational disposition. Candidates should be asked to describe situations where they had to persevere through difficulty, resolve an ethical dilemma, or act in the absence of recognition. The use of the STAR method (Situation, Task, Action, Result) enables evaluators to assess motivational traits such as initiative, integrity, and persistence (Campion et al., 1997). Additionally, agencies can employ psychometric tools such as the *Achievement Motivation Inventory* (AMI) (Schuler & Prochaska, 2001) or the *Work Preference Inventory* (Amabile et al., 1994) to help distinguish between applicants who are intrinsically motivated versus those who are extrinsically motivated. These validated instruments assess dimensions such as preference for challenge, autonomy, recognition, and collaboration, offering a nuanced understanding of motivational drivers that go beyond cognitive ability or personality tests.

Beyond formal testing, agencies should also provide Realistic Job Previews (RJPs) to allow candidates to evaluate the fit between their own values and the actual demands of law enforcement work. Rather than painting an idealized portrait of policing, agencies should present an honest depiction of the role's complexity, emotional demands, bureaucratic challenges, and service expectations. RJPs, delivered through videos, ride-alongs, or interactive simulations, allow applicants to self-assess whether their values and motivations align with the realities of the job. This promotes self-selection, filtering out candidates drawn by glamorized notions of power or excitement, and encouraging those motivated by public service, justice, and personal growth (Wanous, 1992).

Agencies must also consider how they communicate their core values throughout the recruitment process. Mission-centered branding is critical in attracting individuals whose intrinsic motivation aligns with departmental goals. Recruitment materials, including websites, social media, and public engagement events, should emphasize the values of community service, procedural justice, and integrity. The language used, the images shared, and the narratives conveyed all contribute to an implicit message about what the department stands for—and what it rewards. Agencies that consistently highlight service, fairness, and personal growth signal to applicants that they are entering a values-driven profession, not just a job.

Recruiting for motivational fit is not just a matter of personnel quality—it is a strategy for cultural coherence and ethical resilience.

When officers join with intrinsic motivations that align with the organization's mission, they are more likely to engage deeply with training, persist through adversity, and internalize ethical standards. This alignment also enhances long-term organizational outcomes, including reduced turnover, fewer disciplinary issues, and greater community trust (Mastrofski, Willis, & Kochel, 2007). It creates a workforce that is not only capable but committed—a force that sees law enforcement not merely as an occupation, but as a calling rooted in service and responsibility.

In sum, a motivationally attuned recruitment and selection process is the first step in a life-cycle approach to developing high-performing, ethical, and achievement-oriented officers. It sets the tone for a career grounded not just in rules and rewards but in purpose, resilience, and a durable commitment to the principles of democratic policing.

Training for Achievement Orientation in the Academy

Academy environments serve as the crucible in which the foundational beliefs, behaviors, and professional identity of law enforcement officers are formed. These settings are not merely about instilling tactical proficiency or legal knowledge; they are the psychological and moral starting point for an officer's career. Historically, many law enforcement academies have adopted training models rooted in paramilitary structures, emphasizing obedience, control, and rote repetition of procedures. While such methods can effectively produce short-term compliance and uniformity in behavior, they often rely heavily on extrinsic motivators—fear of failure, the pursuit of status, or conformity to hierarchy (Conti & Nolan, 2005). These approaches may unintentionally suppress critical thinking, dampen intrinsic motivation, and risk disengagement among recruits, especially those drawn to policing for service-oriented or ethical reasons.

To produce officers who are resilient, self-directed, and ethically grounded, academies must shift toward pedagogical models that embed the principles of achievement motivation. According to Ryan and Deci's (2000) Self-Determination Theory, three psychological needs—autonomy, competence, and relatedness—are central to sustaining intrinsic motivation. When these needs are met in training environments, officers are more likely to adopt a mastery orientation toward their work, developing a durable internal drive that supports lifelong learning, ethical conduct, and adaptive problem-solving. Embedding these principles early in academy training does not mean abandoning structure or standards, but rather, complementing them with practices that support individual growth, critical engagement, and purposeful service.

One of the most effective methods for cultivating achievement motivation is scenario-based learning. Unlike traditional drills or prescriptive role-play, scenario-based training immerses recruits in dynamic, open-ended situations that mirror the real-world ambiguity and complexity of police work. These exercises require judgment under uncertainty, strategic thinking, ethical discernment, and the integration of multiple competencies—from communication and situational awareness to tactical coordination and legal compliance. This format supports the development of metacognition (the ability to reflect on one's own thinking) and encourages recruits to view challenges as opportunities for growth rather than threats to competence. When properly structured and facilitated, scenario-based learning activates the motivational circuits associated with autonomy and competence, reinforcing the idea that policing is a thinking profession requiring continual learning and adaptation.

Equally important is the integration of reflective practice into the academy experience. While scenario-based learning tests decision-making in real time, reflection enables recruits to make sense of those experiences after the fact. Journaling, guided debriefings, or structured ethical discussions provide trainees with a forum to process their emotional responses, analyze decision outcomes, and connect their actions to their deeper professional values. These activities help bridge the gap between procedural knowledge and moral reasoning, reinforcing the development of an internalized professional identity rooted in service, justice, and accountability. Reflection also supports emotional regulation and stress processing, which are essential for long-term psychological resilience in high-pressure roles.

Another foundational strategy is the use of incremental challenge—deliberately designing a training curriculum that builds complexity over time. Rather than throwing recruits into high-stress situations prematurely or keeping them confined to repetitive basics, instructors should scaffold learning experiences to gradually increase in difficulty, risk, and responsibility. This allows recruits to accumulate what Bandura (1997) referred to as "mastery experiences," which are the most powerful source of self-efficacy. When recruits succeed at progressively more demanding tasks, they come to believe in their ability to meet future challenges, even under conditions of uncertainty or stress. This belief—"I can handle this because I've succeeded before"—is foundational to sustained motivation and effective performance in the field.

Feedback is another cornerstone of motivational development. In traditional models, feedback is often used to correct errors or assert authority, which may breed defensiveness or passive compliance. In contrast, achievement-oriented training emphasizes feedback that is constructive, timely, and specific to the learning goals of the individual. This includes acknowledging effort, recognizing improvement, and encouraging reflection on ethical implications and strategic choices. When instructors frame mistakes as learning opportunities rather than failings, they help maintain psychological safety and reinforce a growth mindset. Over time, this approach cultivates resilient officers who are not only technically competent but also open to feedback, capable of self-assessment, and committed to continuous improvement.

In addition to shaping individual motivation, these practices help build a collective learning culture within the academy. Recruits begin to associate police work not just with compliance and control but with intellectual challenge, ethical service, and personal mastery. They internalize the belief that excellence in policing is achieved not through rigid conformity, but through thoughtful engagement, reflection, and perseverance. This motivational orientation is especially critical in a profession where officers must make autonomous decisions in morally complex environments without immediate supervision.

Collectively, these strategies—scenario-based learning, reflective practice, incremental challenge, and developmental feedback—create a training environment that supports mastery-oriented motivation. Research consistently links this type of motivation to better job satisfaction, increased organizational commitment, reduced ethical erosion, and greater adaptability in complex operational contexts (Kernis & Goldman, 2006; Dweck, 2006). When achievement motivation becomes part of the academy's ethos, recruits leave not only with tactical proficiency but with a psychological foundation for professional excellence and public trust.

Confidence Building Through Simulation and Stress Exposure Training

Achievement-motivated individuals thrive when they are challenged—but only if they believe they can succeed. Confidence, or perceived self-efficacy, is a prerequisite for sustained motivation in high-stakes roles, such as policing (Bandura, 1997). This belief in one's capabilities plays a pivotal role in determining how much effort an officer will exert, how long they will persist in the face of difficulties, and whether they view setbacks as failure or as learning opportunities. Training environments that cultivate confidence without fostering complacency are critical for preparing officers to act decisively, ethically, and competently under pressure. Law enforcement officers often find themselves making life-altering decisions in seconds, and those who possess strong self-efficacy are more likely to make reasoned choices that align with departmental values and public expectations. Simulation-based learning, when paired with deliberate stress inoculation techniques, provides a unique method to simultaneously hone technical proficiency and reinforce motivational resilience.

Tactical Decision Games (TDGs), for example, are highly effective exercises that present trainees with intricate, time-sensitive dilemmas requiring ethical judgment, situational awareness, and tactical precision. These simulations are not limited to rote procedures; rather, they challenge officers to synthesise their training knowledge, assess evolving risks, and respond effectively under cognitive load. In TDGs, recruits learn to navigate gray areas—balancing assertiveness with emotional control and legal constraints with community expectations. They also gain exposure to the types of ambiguity that typify real-world policing. Importantly, TDGs create a safe space for trial and error, allowing officers to experiment with decisions and learn from their missteps without the consequence of real-world failure. This controlled exposure to complexity promotes both decision-making agility and moral reasoning.

Virtual Reality (VR) technology expands the possibilities of immersive training by placing officers in hyper-realistic scenarios that mimic the sensory overload and emotional weight of actual field conditions. Whether the simulation involves de-escalating a domestic disturbance, responding to a suicide threat, or managing a high-risk traffic stop, VR allows trainees to rehearse these critical incidents multiple times, with each iteration building their skills and emotional regulation. The visual, auditory, and kinesthetic realism of VR enhances cognitive processing and memory encoding, making it more likely that learned behaviors will transfer to real-world settings. Moreover, VR allows instructors to introduce variables—such as bystander reactions or unpredictable subject behavior—that require officers to adapt quickly and think on their feet, reinforcing adaptability as a core professional trait.

After-Action Reviews (AARs) following simulations are equally essential for internalizing lessons and reinforcing a growth-oriented mindset. Effective AARs go beyond listing what went wrong; they explore the underlying thought processes, emotional reactions, and moral judgments that contributed to those decisions. By facilitating these reviews with empathy and curiosity rather than judgment, instructors help trainees reflect more deeply on their motivations and choices. This process fosters metacognitive awareness—understanding one's own thinking—and enhances emotional intelligence, both of which are linked to ethical resilience and long-term job satisfaction. When feedback is constructive, timely, and connected to learning goals, it preserves motivational momentum and prevents defensive reactions or withdrawal.

Equally important to the training environment is the behavior and presence of instructors. When academy staff consistently model calmness under pressure, articulate their ethical reasoning during simulations, and provide steady, personalized encouragement, they embody the standards they expect of recruits. These instructors become more than just teachers—they become living examples of the professional identity the agency seeks to instill. Their conduct communicates that ethical conduct, emotional regulation, and intellectual humility are not just aspirational traits but practical necessities for effective policing.

Ultimately, simulation and stress exposure training accomplish far more than technical readiness. They embed foundational beliefs about challenge, accountability, and personal growth that define how officers respond to adversity throughout their careers. These formative experiences help shape a motivational architecture rooted in self-efficacy, resilience, and a sense of purpose. Officers who undergo such training are better equipped to maintain composure in volatile situations, adapt to new challenges, and remain committed to public service values in the face of adversity. In doing so, they become not only more capable professionals but also more grounded and motivated public servants.

Post-Academy: Mentorship and Motivational Continuity

The transition from the academy to field training is a critical juncture where motivational gains can be either reinforced or lost. This period is a crucible for shaping long-term professional identity, and the influence of Field Training Officers (FTOs) cannot be overstated. FTOs are not just role models for technical proficiency; they are the bridge between formal instruction and real-world policing. The quality and disposition of these mentors significantly shape how recruits interpret their role in terms of purpose, autonomy, and ethical decision-making (Chappell, 2007).

Departments must adopt a deliberate strategy when selecting and preparing FTOs. It is not enough to appoint individuals based solely on tenure or tactical competence. Ideal FTOs should embody a high degree of achievement motivation, demonstrate emotional intelligence, and possess exceptional interpersonal communication skills. They must be capable of guiding new officers not only through the mechanics of police work but also through the emotional and moral complexities of the profession. To this end, agencies should provide FTOs with targeted training in mentorship, motivational interviewing, and adult learning principles. These tools allow mentors to reinforce internal motivation, promote reflection, and cultivate a growth mindset.

Additionally, the implementation of structured feedback systems is essential. These systems should evaluate not just technical performance but also motivational health, ethical development, and adaptability. Regular check-ins with recruits during and after their FTO period can help identify early signs of disengagement or ethical conflict. When recruits transition into a motivationally supportive work environment, they are more likely to retain the values and psychological growth cultivated during the academy. Conversely, exposure to toxic subcultures or indifferent supervisors can quickly erode morale and ethical orientation (Reiner, 2010).

Advanced Training and Lifelong Learning

Motivation does not plateau after the academy—it must be sustained, renewed, and adapted as officers progress through different stages of their careers. However, many departments treat training as a series of isolated events, often tied to certification requirements or reactive responses to operational needs. This episodic model neglects the importance of motivational continuity and leaves officers vulnerable to stagnation, cynicism, and burnout, particularly during mid-career transitions (Maslach & Leiter, 2016).

To foster enduring motivation, agencies must design professional development systems that are both structured and flexible, allowing officers to chart paths aligned with their evolving interests and strengths. Tiered training frameworks should offer progression opportunities in areas such as crisis negotiation, community engagement, tactical operations, or technology-enabled investigations. When officers are able to specialize in domains that align with their motivational profile—particularly the need for achievement (nAch)—they are more likely to remain engaged and committed to high standards of performance.

Leadership development should also be reimagined as a continuous process that extends beyond technical training. Programs must integrate emotional intelligence, ethical leadership, and motivational psychology, cultivating leaders who inspire others and serve as cultural anchors within their agencies (Brown & Treviño, 2006). Promotion should not signal the end of learning but the beginning of a new phase of growth and responsibility.

Furthermore, departments should actively support partnerships with institutions of higher education. These collaborations can facilitate access to degree programs, certificate courses, and specialized training in ethics, organizational behavior, and public administration. By integrating academic learning with field experience, officers develop critical thinking skills, reflective capacity, and a broader understanding of their role in a democratic society.

Ultimately, lifelong learning reinforces the identity of an officer as a dynamic, evolving professional. It signals that growth is not limited to the early years of service but is a continual pursuit grounded in the values of service, justice, and excellence (Kolb, 1984). Such a culture not only sustains motivation but also prepares agencies to meet the complex and shifting demands of modern policing.

Conclusion

Motivational development should be a deliberate and strategic goal embedded into every phase of law enforcement training, from initial recruitment through to retirement. Motivation is not an incidental byproduct of police training; it is a vital outcome that must be cultivated, monitored, and reinforced across the career lifespan. By intentionally aligning training methodologies with well-established psychological theories—particularly McClelland's (1961) theory of achievement motivation—departments can foster the internal drive that supports not just technical competence, but ethical behavior, professional resilience, and a sustained commitment to public service.

When agencies invest in training that nurtures autonomy, purpose, and a growth mindset, they develop officers who are not only better performers but also more adaptive, ethical, and emotionally intelligent. This begins with the recruitment process, where motivational fit must be considered alongside aptitude and background checks. It continues in the academy, where scenario-based learning, reflective practice, and incremental challenge instill a mastery-oriented mindset. It is further reinforced in field training through motivationally attuned mentorship, and throughout an officer's career via opportunities for specialization, higher education, and leadership development.

Importantly, this approach requires a paradigm shift—from episodic, compliance-driven training focused on minimum standards to a model of continuous professional and personal development. Such a model honors officers not just as enforcers of the law, but as learners, leaders, and moral agents within the communities they serve. Departments that adopt this mindset are not only building skills—they are cultivating the spirit of public service that forms the bedrock of legitimacy and trust in democratic policing.

Ultimately, training for motivation is not a luxury—it is a necessity. In an era of complex social dynamics, increased scrutiny, and evolving threats, law enforcement agencies must prepare their officers not only to act, but to act with integrity, insight, and a deep sense of purpose. By doing so, they ensure that the profession remains not only effective, but honorable, sustainable, and worthy of the public's trust.

Chapter 11: Motivation Across Borders: International Policing Perspectives

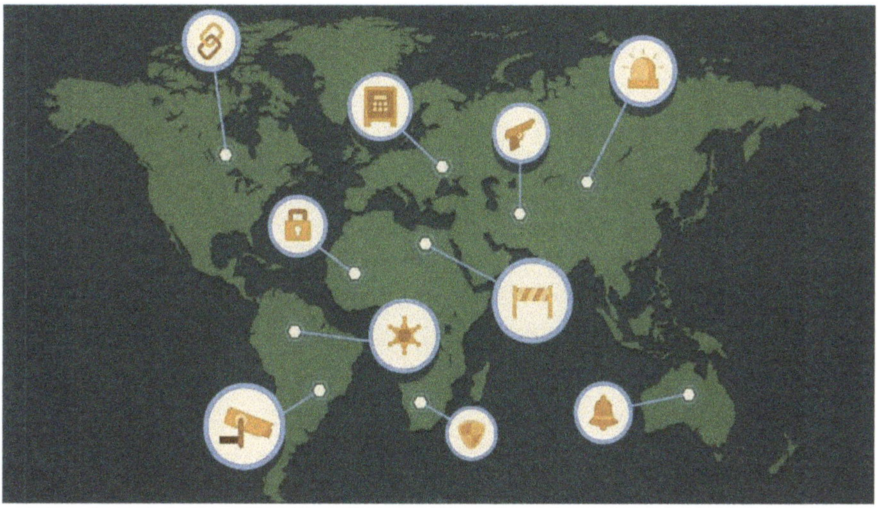

Introduction

In an era of increasing globalization, transnational crime, and international police cooperation, understanding the motivational dynamics of law enforcement professionals across different cultural contexts is more important than ever. While policing universally involves managing public order, enforcing laws, and ensuring community safety, the motivational structures that drive officer behavior are deeply influenced by political systems, cultural values, historical experiences, and institutional frameworks. This chapter explores how achievement motivation, as defined by McClelland (1961), manifests across diverse international policing environments. It examines case studies from various countries, identifies cross-cultural differences and commonalities in motivational expression, and distills lessons from international police academies and leadership development programs.

Understanding motivation in international policing is essential for several reasons. First, it informs the development of culturally sensitive leadership models that recognize and respect local values while promoting professional excellence. Second, it enhances the effectiveness of international training collaborations by ensuring that instructional methods align with the motivational profiles of participating officers. Third, it contributes to reform initiatives in developing or transitional states where police legitimacy, morale, and accountability often face serious challenges.

Policing systems across the globe vary in structure, ethos, and operational mandates. In Scandinavian countries, for example, policing tends to emphasize community engagement, social equity, and high levels of educational attainment among officers, often attracting individuals with a strong intrinsic motivation for public service. In contrast, some authoritarian regimes may reward loyalty to the state or political party over merit, fostering extrinsic motivation tied to job security or status rather than service to the public. These differences matter because they shape how officers perceive their roles, how they respond to ethical dilemmas, and how they interpret performance standards.

Achievement motivation (nAch), as conceptualized by McClelland, remains a valuable lens through which to analyze these variations. In some systems, high nAch is supported by transparent promotion pathways, performance recognition, and training programs that reward innovation and critical thinking. In others, where hierarchy and conformity are prioritized, nAch may be stifled, leading to compliance-based behavior rather than principled initiative. Understanding these dynamics allows reformers, trainers, and policymakers to design motivationally appropriate interventions that resonate across borders.

This chapter draws from qualitative and quantitative research, field assessments, and practitioner insights to examine how motivation is developed, expressed, and sustained in law enforcement settings from Latin America to Europe, Africa, and Asia. By comparing institutional structures, academy models, and leadership practices, it seeks to identify both the cultural anchors of motivation and the universal principles that support ethical, committed, and high-performing police forces.

Achievement Motivation in Cross-Cultural Contexts

David McClelland's Three Needs Theory—comprising the need for achievement (nAch), affiliation (nAff), and power (nPow)—offers a powerful lens for examining how motivation operates within different policing systems. However, cross-cultural psychology warns against assuming uniform expression of these needs. Hofstede's (2001) cultural dimensions theory suggests that societies vary in their orientations toward individualism, power distance, uncertainty avoidance, and long-term orientation—all of which influence how motivational traits are nurtured or constrained.

For instance, in individualistic cultures such as the United States or the United Kingdom, nAch may be expressed through personal initiative, competitive performance evaluations, and professional advancement. Officers in these contexts are often encouraged to stand out, pursue specialized roles, and innovate. Leadership in such systems tends to reward innovation, initiative, and strong performance metrics, with an emphasis on individual accountability. Motivation is driven by personal goals, the pursuit of distinction, and recognition of one's unique contributions to the organization.

In contrast, collectivist cultures, such as those in Japan or South Korea, may channel achievement motivation through group loyalty, team-based outcomes, and institutional conformity. Here, individual ambition is often subordinated to the success of the unit or department, and motivation is reinforced through communal identity and hierarchical approval. Officers are expected to prioritize harmony, follow protocol, and maintain respect for tradition. The success of the group, rather than the individual, is often the ultimate metric of achievement, and motivation stems from contributing to shared goals and earning collective respect.

Power distance is another critical variable. In low power distance societies (e.g., the Netherlands, Sweden), officers may feel empowered to question authority, engage in collaborative decision-making, and innovate from the bottom up. Achievement motivation in such settings may be driven by autonomy and mutual accountability. Officers are encouraged to be self-starters, engage in community-based decision-making, and seek peer validation.

Conversely, in high power distance societies (e.g., India, Mexico), motivation is more likely to be linked with status, formal recognition, and upward mobility within rigid hierarchies. Promotion may depend more on seniority or deference to rank than on innovation or peer consensus. Officers in such systems often derive motivation from clear authority structures and a defined path to leadership. Superiors are expected to model excellence, and motivation is reinforced by institutional hierarchy and formal commendation.

These cultural patterns shape not only how leadership is exercised, but also how officers interpret the value of their contributions. Understanding these nuances is essential for international collaborations, reform efforts, and leadership development programs. Training that ignores these cultural dimensions may inadvertently undermine local motivation systems or fail to produce the desired behavioral change. Thus, international policing initiatives must consider the interplay between motivational theory and cultural context to build sustainable and culturally coherent professional development frameworks.

Case Studies in Motivational Expression

United Kingdom: Policing Through Legitimacy and Procedural Justice

British policing, particularly in England and Wales, has historically emphasized legitimacy and procedural justice as cornerstones of officer motivation and public trust. The College of Policing has strategically embedded achievement motivation within its National Policing Curriculum, highlighting ethical decision-making, community engagement, and reflective practice as core competencies (College of Policing, 2019). Officers are evaluated not solely on traditional performance metrics, such as arrests or case closures, but also on how professionally and ethically they carry out their duties. This approach reinforces the motivational connection between personal competence and ethical behavior. Tools such as body-worn cameras enhance accountability and transparency, while specialized community liaison roles offer officers the opportunity to build long-term, trust-based relationships with citizens. Additionally, structured career progression systems encourage goal orientation and mastery by providing clear benchmarks for professional advancement.

Japan: Achievement Through Discipline and Group Identity

Japan's police system reflects a cultural synthesis of achievement motivation with collectivist values, resulting in a highly disciplined and hierarchical organization. Police academies in Japan subject recruits to rigorous training regimens that emphasize not only technical skill but also social harmony, group loyalty, and moral conduct. Achievement is not defined in individualistic terms but through the enhancement of the department's collective reputation and societal standing. Officers are expected to internalize group norms and maintain high standards of behavior, both in public and within their units. Shared living arrangements during academy training, communal rituals, and regular rotational assignments across different units further reinforce a sense of shared mission and group cohesion. These practices embed motivation in a context where conformity, attention to detail, and collective pride fuel professional performance (Bayley, 1991).

Germany: Competence-Driven Professionalism

Germany's decentralized federal police model fosters both regional autonomy and nationwide professional consistency. Achievement motivation is cultivated through a meritocratic system that values educational qualifications, cognitive capability, and ethical discernment. Entry into the police force often requires completion of higher secondary education (Abitur) or a university-level degree, signaling an emphasis on intellectual and moral preparedness. Once recruited, officers undergo systematic training that integrates legal instruction, tactical proficiency, and psychological resilience. German police academies emphasize scenario-based simulations that replicate real-life moral dilemmas, promoting the development of critical thinking, emotional regulation, and principled judgment. Continuous professional development and structured mentorship programs are institutionalized, allowing officers to refine their skills and maintain high motivational standards throughout their careers. These measures reflect a national ethos that equates public trust with demonstrable competence and ethical consistency (Waddington & Wright, 2008).

Colombia: Motivation in the Context of Transformation

Colombia provides a unique lens through which to understand motivational development in the aftermath of political violence and institutional mistrust. Following decades of armed conflict, the Colombian National Police (CNP) has undergone comprehensive reform, transitioning from a militarized, reactive force to a community-focused and human rights–centered institution. This transformation was achieved through international partnerships with organizations such as the United Nations Office on Drugs and Crime (UNODC) and the International Criminal Investigative Training Assistance Program (ICITAP), which supported efforts to embed values of ethical leadership, accountability, and trauma-informed service into training curricula. Officers are now educated in areas such as peacebuilding, transitional justice, community reconciliation, and psychological resilience. This shift reflects a redefined motivational structure in which personal fulfillment and professional achievement stem from service to vulnerable populations and the rebuilding of public legitimacy. Through its reorientation toward ethics and humanity, Colombia illustrates how achievement motivation can be reawakened and redirected to support national healing and social cohesion (UNODC, 2021).

Cross-Cultural Considerations in Leadership Development

Leadership development programs must be culturally attuned if they are to effectively support motivation, particularly when working across diverse policing systems. Programs designed in one national or institutional context may not seamlessly transfer to another due to differing values, communication styles, and organizational norms. Strategies that emphasize autonomy, decentralized decision-making, and egalitarian team structures may thrive in cultures that value individualism and low power distance, such as Canada, the Netherlands, or Australia. However, these same strategies may falter in more hierarchical societies, where respect for authority, protocol, and chain of command is deeply embedded.

Conversely, leadership models based on status recognition, ritualized respect, and symbolic authority may resonate more strongly in traditional or collectivist contexts, such as those found in many countries in Asia, Africa, or Latin America. In these environments, leaders are often expected to embody institutional prestige, moral authority, and protective paternalism. Failure to recognize these cultural expectations can lead to resistance or disengagement from leadership development initiatives, even when their content is otherwise sound.

Research by Den Hartog et al. (1999) in the GLOBE study—an influential cross-cultural research project examining leadership and organizational behavior across 62 societies—provides insight into this complexity. The study found that certain leadership attributes, such as integrity, decisiveness, and fairness, were universally endorsed as effective. However, the expression and reinforcement of these traits differed. In Latin American cultures, for instance, mentorship, relational warmth, and face-to-face rapport were found to be critical for leader credibility and influence. Leaders are often judged by their interpersonal grace as much as their technical expertise. In contrast, in many Northern European cultures, motivational influence is more strongly associated with formal certification, procedural consistency, and demonstrated technical mastery.

Effective leadership training must therefore strike a balance between global best practices and localized cultural understanding. Programs should adapt curriculum design to reflect cultural attitudes toward hierarchy, authority, and collaboration. This could involve restructuring exercises to emphasize group consensus in collectivist cultures or reinforcing individual initiative in more individualistic societies. Language and symbols used in training materials should align with cultural values—for example, using metaphors of family or harmony in collectivist settings and metaphors of competition or personal growth in individualistic settings.

Additionally, leadership development must incorporate culturally specific role models and real-life case studies that reflect the local law enforcement landscape. Officers are more likely to be motivated by leadership lessons that feel authentic and attainable within their institutional setting. Self-assessment tools and reflective exercises should be tailored to include cultural definitions of achievement and success, acknowledging that what constitutes "excellence" or "leadership potential" may vary across cultural contexts.

Ultimately, culturally competent leadership development not only supports the motivational needs of individual officers but also strengthens organizational legitimacy. When officers see leadership training as relevant to their lived experiences and institutional challenges, they are more likely to internalize its lessons and translate them into practice. This enhances not just personal growth but collective efficacy—crucial for law enforcement agencies navigating the complexities of globalized public safety.

Lessons from International Police Academies

Despite wide variation in institutional structure, cultural values, and legal frameworks, several shared practices emerge from international police training systems that support and reinforce motivational development in law enforcement professionals. These practices reflect a growing recognition that effective policing requires more than tactical proficiency—it demands ethical engagement, emotional resilience, and a sustained sense of purpose. The following strategies have proven especially effective in fostering achievement-oriented mindsets across diverse contexts:

1. *Values-Based Curriculum:* Increasingly, police academies worldwide are embedding human rights, ethical decision-making, and cultural competence into their foundational training. In Scandinavian countries, for example, cadets study democratic policing models and procedural justice as part of their core curriculum, reinforcing internalized motivation through moral engagement. These modules help recruits understand the broader societal role of policing and cultivate a sense of ethical identity that aligns with public service values. By framing law enforcement as a vocation rooted in justice and equity, values-based curricula shift motivational emphasis from mere compliance to principled performance.

2. *Scenario-Driven Pedagogy:* Scenario-based learning has become a cornerstone of police education across Europe, Asia, and the Americas. In Germany and the Netherlands, trainees regularly participate in simulated environments that test their ability to de-escalate conflict, assess threats, and navigate complex legal and ethical dilemmas. These scenarios are not just tactical drills—they are opportunities to develop reflective judgment, emotional control, and adaptive reasoning. In South Korea and Japan, scenario-based training is combined with rigorous feedback protocols and peer evaluation, reinforcing a mastery-oriented culture. This experiential approach engages achievement motivation by challenging recruits to problem-solve creatively and perform under pressure, all while maintaining ethical clarity.

3. *Mentorship and Career Mapping:* A recurring feature of successful international systems is the early and ongoing use of mentorship. In Canada and Australia, for instance, recruits are paired with seasoned officers who model professional behavior, provide emotional support, and guide

developmental feedback. This relational scaffolding is often accompanied by transparent career pathways that align achievement motivation with institutional commitment. Officers are encouraged to pursue specialization, leadership development, and advanced education, allowing them to envision a fulfilling and impactful career trajectory. Clear advancement opportunities reduce attrition, foster organizational loyalty, and sustain motivation beyond the academy.

4. *Psychological Resilience Training:* Recognizing the emotional demands of law enforcement, many police academies have begun incorporating psychological wellness and resilience into their curricula. In Colombia, post-conflict policing reforms have emphasized trauma-informed training and emotional regulation to rebuild trust and internal motivation. In Canada, resilience programs include mindfulness, stress inoculation, and peer-led wellness circles, helping recruits manage anxiety and remain emotionally present. German academies integrate modules on emotional intelligence, moral injury, and burnout prevention, framing mental wellness as a cornerstone of professional excellence. These initiatives support long-term motivational sustainability by protecting officers from the erosion of purpose caused by cumulative stress.

Together, these strategies suggest that regardless of national culture, officers benefit from training environments that connect competence with meaning, and autonomy with accountability. International police academies that embrace values-based learning, experiential pedagogy, structured mentorship, and psychological wellness are better equipped to produce officers who are not only skilled but also intrinsically motivated, ethically grounded, and resilient in the face of complexity. These shared practices offer a blueprint for global policing systems committed to excellence, legitimacy, and sustained public trust.

Conclusion

Motivation in policing is not a monolithic concept—it is a culturally conditioned construct that is shaped by national values, institutional histories, and societal expectations. Yet, despite these differences, the fundamental psychological drivers of achievement motivation as theorized by McClelland (1961)—the need for achievement, power, and affiliation—remain remarkably consistent across global policing systems. Officers everywhere are influenced by how well their environments support their personal and professional aspirations. Whether serving in a collectivist society like Japan or a more individualistic one like the United States, the universal human desire to perform meaningful work, to develop competence, and to contribute to something larger than oneself provides a common motivational foundation.

Understanding this intersection between culture and psychology is essential for designing training systems that do more than teach tactics—they must cultivate identity, resilience, and ethical decision-making. As demonstrated in case studies from countries such as the United Kingdom, Germany, Colombia, and Japan, the expression of motivation may vary, but the need to nurture it through structured, values-based environments remains the same. From the inclusion of moral philosophy and human rights in academy curricula to the deployment of mentorship and psychological support programs, global police training institutions have shown that motivation is not a static trait but a developmental outcome.

Moreover, culturally competent leadership plays a pivotal role in sustaining officer motivation across borders. Leaders who are attuned to local norms and who integrate global best practices into locally relevant training frameworks can create environments where achievement motivation flourishes. By acknowledging the influence of power distance, individualism, uncertainty avoidance, and other cultural dimensions (Hofstede, 2001), law enforcement agencies can build leadership pipelines that are inclusive, ethical, and motivationally strategic. Leadership development that recognizes diverse pathways to excellence—and respects how different cultures interpret success, authority, and service—can unify international policing efforts around shared professional ideals.

Ultimately, the motivation to serve, excel, and act with integrity is a universal aspiration that transcends jurisdictional boundaries. By investing in the motivational health of their officers—through training, support, and leadership—law enforcement agencies worldwide can enhance both internal performance and public legitimacy. In a time when global security challenges demand cross-border cooperation, the ability to understand and support motivation across cultures is not merely advantageous—it is foundational to building trust, promoting justice, and advancing the professionalism of policing on the world stage.

Chapter 12: The Future of Motivation in Policing

Introduction

As policing continues to evolve in response to emerging social, technological, and institutional challenges, the question of what sustains officer commitment, ethical conduct, and operational excellence becomes increasingly urgent. Traditional models of law enforcement, long anchored in command-and-control paradigms and reactive deployment, are proving insufficient to meet the complexity of 21st-century demands. In this context, the future of policing cannot be shaped solely by tactical innovation, algorithmic surveillance, or legal reform; it must also be rooted in a nuanced understanding of human behavior—specifically, the psychology of motivation.

Motivation is no longer a peripheral concern or the sole domain of personnel managers. It is a strategic resource—one that influences recruitment outcomes, organizational culture, community trust, and officer resilience. The future of policing requires a paradigmatic shift in how departments conceptualize and cultivate this resource. Rather than treating motivation as a fixed trait or merely a response to incentives, forward-looking agencies must view it as a dynamic and malleable capability that can be nurtured through deliberate interventions at all stages of the policing lifecycle.

Drawing from foundational theories such as David McClelland's Three Needs Theory (1961), which emphasizes the need for achievement (nAch), affiliation (nAff), and power (nPow), as well as Self-Determination Theory (Ryan & Deci, 2000), which distinguishes between intrinsic and extrinsic motivational forces, this chapter explores how motivational science can guide the design of holistic law enforcement systems. These theories offer powerful frameworks to understand why officers enter the profession, how they respond to institutional pressures, and what sustains their engagement over time. Furthermore, insights from occupational psychology, including constructs like psychological capital (Luthans et al., 2007), job crafting (Wrzesniewski & Dutton, 2001), and motivational fit, provide tools for designing environments that optimize individual strengths within collective missions.

This chapter argues that future-ready law enforcement organizations will be those that systematically integrate motivational principles into every layer of their operations—from recruitment and selection to training, leadership development, policy formulation, and organizational innovation. By embedding motivation into structural frameworks, agencies can not only predict and enhance performance but also address long-standing challenges such as officer burnout, attrition, misconduct, and disengagement. Ultimately, the most resilient officers and effective organizations will be those that serve not just because they are assigned, but because they are driven.

Motivational Science and Recruitment

As law enforcement agencies face increasing demands for accountability, emotional intelligence, and cultural competence, the process of recruiting new officers must evolve to prioritize not only competence but motivational alignment. Historically, recruitment has centered on observable qualifications—such as physical endurance, cognitive aptitude, background integrity, and basic legal knowledge. While these factors remain important, they are insufficient predictors of ethical resilience, discretionary judgment, and long-term engagement. The future of effective recruitment lies in the science of motivation: understanding what drives individuals to join law enforcement, and more importantly, what sustains them in the face of adversity.

Motivational fit refers to the congruence between an individual's core psychological drivers and the demands and values of the organization they join. Officers who are intrinsically motivated—those whose behavior is fueled by internalized values such as service, justice, mastery, and community responsibility—are significantly more likely to engage in ethical conduct, adapt to stress, and exhibit greater commitment across their careers (Van Gelderen, Van der Veen, & Verkleij, 2011). In contrast, candidates driven primarily by extrinsic motivators—such as job security, authority, or salary—may be more susceptible to disillusionment, rule-bending, or disengagement when external rewards are removed or questioned (Ryan & Deci, 2000).

To assess motivational orientation systematically, departments should integrate validated psychometric tools into their recruitment protocols. Instruments such as the Achievement Motivation Inventory (AMI) (Schuler & Prochaska, 2001) can measure dimensions including persistence, goal orientation, and preference for difficult tasks—indicators of high nAch (need for achievement). The Work Preference Inventory (WPI) (Amabile et al., 1994) distinguishes between intrinsic and extrinsic motivational styles, providing insight into whether applicants are more likely to pursue excellence for its own sake or for external validation. These tools, when used ethically and in conjunction with behavioral interviews and scenario-based assessments, allow agencies to screen not just for risk, but for alignment with the deeper mission of public service.

Moreover, recruitment messaging itself must be recalibrated to attract candidates whose motivational structures resonate with the evolving goals of democratic policing. Traditional recruitment slogans emphasizing excitement, authority, or combat readiness may unintentionally appeal to those high in personalized power (nPow) rather than socialized leadership. Instead, future campaigns should foreground values such as ethical challenge, meaningful public engagement, restorative problem-solving, and professional growth. Highlighting opportunities for mentorship, community impact, and specialized skill development can help signal to applicants that law enforcement is not just a job—it is a calling rooted in societal service and individual purpose.

In sum, motivational science offers law enforcement a proactive strategy to select candidates not only with the capacity to succeed, but with the character and drive to thrive. By investing in recruitment practices that prioritize internal alignment with institutional mission and community values, policing agencies lay the foundation for a more motivated, accountable, and resilient workforce.

Policy Development through a Motivational Lens

Traditionally, policy within law enforcement has been conceived as a tool for standardization, control, and legal compliance—written rules designed to constrain behavior and ensure consistency across officers and operations. While this regulatory function is essential, it reflects a narrow view of human behavior that emphasizes external control over internal motivation. In contrast, emerging research in organizational behavior and motivation science suggests that policies can serve as powerful psychological instruments—tools that shape values, influence morale, and guide discretionary effort when thoughtfully constructed.

When policies are overly punitive, overly prescriptive, or devoid of human-centered design, they can inadvertently undermine motivation. Such rigid frameworks may trigger psychological reactance—a motivational state in which individuals resist control or mandates that limit their perceived autonomy (Brehm, 1966). In policing, this can manifest as rule circumvention, passive compliance, or disengagement from the spirit of the law.

Conversely, when policies are framed to support intrinsic motivation—such as through language that reinforces professional purpose, autonomy, and ethical competence—they can inspire commitment rather than merely enforce obedience.

One of the most impactful areas for motivationally attuned policy is performance evaluation. Systems that narrowly measure output—such as arrest quotas, citations issued, or calls handled—may unintentionally promote counterproductive behaviors like "gaming the system" or prioritizing quantity over quality (Anechiarico & Jacobs, 1996). These output-based systems risk reinforcing extrinsic motivation, which can erode ethical sensitivity and long-term engagement. In contrast, policies that reward ethical initiative, problem-solving creativity, community collaboration, and reflective judgment foster what Kernis and Goldman (2006) describe as authentic functioning—a motivational state where behavior aligns with personal values and professional standards.

Furthermore, policies should promote feedback loops and participatory input. When officers are given a voice in shaping or refining departmental policies—through advisory committees, post-incident reviews, or policy testing pilots—they are more likely to perceive those policies as legitimate, just, and worthy of adherence (Tyler & Huo, 2002). This sense of procedural fairness enhances both compliance and motivation, as officers feel recognized not only as enforcers but as contributors to organizational knowledge and justice.

Another underutilized area is policy-based recognition frameworks. Institutions can design internal policies that formalize recognition for non-traditional forms of excellence, such as peer support, conflict de-escalation, community relationship-building, or mentoring. By embedding symbolic and material recognition into policy language and promotion criteria, departments send a clear message about what is valued. These signals have a profound impact on motivation, particularly among high-achievement officers who seek purposeful mastery and internal validation.

Ultimately, viewing policy through a motivational lens transforms it from a reactive tool of control into a proactive mechanism for professional development, cultural shaping, and psychological alignment. Law enforcement leaders and policymakers must therefore collaborate with behavioral scientists, ethics scholars, and line officers to co-create policies that inspire, not just instruct. In doing so, they not only regulate conduct—they elevate it.

Training Innovation and Lifelong Development

As policing enters an era defined by complexity, public scrutiny, and rapidly evolving challenges, the future of training must prioritize not only technical proficiency but also the development and sustainability of officer motivation. Motivation is not a static trait embedded during academy instruction—it is a dynamic construct that evolves across the career span. To cultivate long-term commitment, resilience, and ethical excellence, law enforcement agencies must adopt training paradigms that are psychologically informed, developmentally sequenced, and technologically adaptive.

A key principle in this transformation is recognizing that scenario-based learning, ethical reflection, stress inoculation, and growth-oriented feedback are no longer supplementary strategies—they are foundational. Research from Bandura (1997) underscores the role of self-efficacy in motivation: officers must believe they can master challenges before they will persist in facing them. Scenario-based training provides precisely this opportunity by immersing officers in realistic, ambiguous, and ethically complex situations that demand more than rote tactics—they require judgment, empathy, discretion, and accountability. These simulations support metacognitive development and strengthen the intrinsic connection between professional decisions and their societal impact.

In parallel, ethical reflection and debriefing—especially when facilitated by instructors trained in motivational theory—help officers internalize learning in a way that reinforces their sense of moral identity and service orientation. Reflective practices, such as journaling, narrative storytelling, and after-action reviews, have been shown to increase ethical awareness, improve emotional regulation, and support the development of a values-based professional self-concept (Kolb, 1984; McAdams, 2001). Stress inoculation training further contributes by preparing officers to maintain motivation under emotional duress, enhancing both performance and psychological resilience in high-pressure environments.

However, to maintain relevance and motivational continuity, training must be ongoing, adaptive, and personalized. The days of episodic, one-size-fits-all in-service training are insufficient for a workforce expected to operate in unpredictable, multicultural, and technologically mediated environments. Leveraging adaptive learning technologies, such as AI-powered simulations, wearable biofeedback tools, and digital competency dashboards, allows agencies to tailor training modules to the specific developmental needs, learning styles, and motivational profiles of individual officers. These platforms can assess an officer's progress in real time, offer targeted feedback, and adjust the difficulty or focus of scenarios to optimize growth. In doing so, they not only improve skill acquisition—they enhance learning motivation by sustaining challenge, relevance, and mastery.

The institutionalization of lifelong learning pathways is equally critical. Departments should establish formal mechanisms that recognize and reward ongoing professional development. This includes offering tuition assistance for higher education, providing leadership and specialization tracks linked to motivational strengths (e.g., negotiation, investigation, community liaison), and integrating career mapping tools that help officers envision a trajectory of impact and growth. By embedding development into promotion criteria and recognition systems, agencies send a powerful signal: learning is not remedial—it is aspirational. Officers are not only permitted but expected to evolve throughout their careers.

Such a system transforms the officer's identity from a technician executing rules to a dynamic professional engaged in a career of service, reflection, and mastery. This redefinition has profound motivational consequences. It affirms that officers are not merely instruments of state power—they are empowered agents of justice, growth, and ethical leadership. In this model, training is no longer a checkpoint—it is a motivational engine that drives excellence across the arc of a policing career.

Retention and Performance Prediction

Policing, like many public service professions, faces persistent challenges in retaining qualified personnel and ensuring consistent performance across an officer's career. High turnover, mid-career burnout, and uneven levels of ethical and tactical performance continue to affect law enforcement agencies worldwide. Motivational science offers a valuable framework for addressing these challenges, not only by helping agencies better understand why officers leave but also by providing actionable tools to predict and enhance long-term engagement and professional excellence.

Research in occupational psychology consistently demonstrates that individuals are more likely to remain in their roles when they perceive a strong alignment between their intrinsic values and the organization's mission (Maslach & Leiter, 2016; Van den Broeck et al., 2010). In the context of policing, officers who are motivated by justice, public service, and ethical integrity are more likely to experience job satisfaction when departmental policies and leadership reflect those same principles. Conversely, when officers feel that organizational priorities are misaligned with their own sense of purpose—such as when the focus is overly punitive, bureaucratic, or disconnected from community needs—disengagement, cynicism, and attrition are likely outcomes.

To proactively manage motivation across the career lifecycle, agencies should implement longitudinal motivational monitoring systems. This can be achieved through a combination of tools, including periodic self-assessments of motivational orientation (e.g., Achievement Motivation Inventory), 360-degree peer feedback, and developmentally focused supervisor evaluations that go beyond technical performance to assess engagement, ethical reasoning, and psychological well-being. These data points can create individual motivational profiles, which serve as early indicators of burnout, stagnation, or misalignment with the organizational culture.

Importantly, these motivational data can be integrated into predictive analytics systems that enhance decision-making at the organizational level. For instance, machine learning algorithms trained on historical data can detect patterns linking motivational decline to turnover, disciplinary infractions, or declines in community engagement scores. When combined with traditional metrics (such as absenteeism, complaint frequency, or productivity drops), motivational indicators can improve the precision of early warning systems, allowing for targeted interventions such as coaching, mentorship, or reassignment before crisis points are reached.

Moreover, motivational profiles can inform succession planning and leadership development. Officers who demonstrate sustained intrinsic motivation—especially achievement-oriented traits such as ethical initiative, reflective learning, and community impact—should be prioritized for future supervisory and command roles. This not only strengthens leadership pipelines but ensures that future leaders possess the internalized commitment and motivational maturity necessary to guide others with integrity and vision.

Another application lies in workforce optimization and task alignment. Matching officers to roles that resonate with their motivational strengths (e.g., assigning high-nAch officers to investigative units or training, placing high-nAff officers in community liaison roles) enhances both satisfaction and performance. Motivation-based assignment systems, supported by data analytics, allow for more strategic personnel deployment and reduce the risk of role misfit, which is a common contributor to both turnover and suboptimal job performance (Kristof-Brown et al., 2005).

Ultimately, retention and performance are not simply matters of compensation, discipline, or policy—they are deeply human and psychological phenomena. Agencies that integrate motivational science into their operational and strategic planning will not only reduce costly turnover but also cultivate a workforce that is motivated, ethical, and prepared to meet the evolving demands of 21st-century policing.

The Role of Leadership and Organizational Culture

No exploration of motivation in policing—present or future—can be complete without a direct focus on the pivotal roles played by leadership and organizational culture. While recruitment tools, training innovations, and policy frameworks shape the contours of a motivationally rich workplace, it is ultimately the behavior and philosophy of leaders that activate or suppress those motivational structures. Leaders set the emotional tone of the agency, model its ethical climate, and create the relational context in which motivation is either nurtured or eroded. In this sense, leadership is not a peripheral concern in motivational development—it is the engine.

Motivationally attuned leaders possess a distinct set of competencies that go beyond technical proficiency or tactical decision-making. They understand and apply principles of motivational science in daily interactions—recognizing that officers, like all employees, respond to environments where their psychological needs for autonomy, competence, and relatedness are met (Ryan & Deci, 2000). These leaders model ethical integrity, articulate a compelling vision of public service, and build climates where officers feel psychologically safe, professionally respected, and emotionally supported (Brown & Treviño, 2006).

To build such leaders systematically, law enforcement agencies must rethink how they design and deliver leadership development programs. Rather than focusing solely on command-and-control paradigms, such programs must integrate motivational diagnostics, emotional intelligence training, and coaching techniques. Supervisors should be trained to recognize signs of burnout, disengagement, or motivational misalignment—and to respond with empathy, developmental feedback, and role reconfiguration when appropriate. The ability to assess and adapt to an officer's motivational state must be considered as essential as the ability to manage crime scenes or deploy resources.

Equally critical is the intentional shaping of organizational culture. Culture is the "unwritten curriculum" of any agency—the shared beliefs, norms, and values that guide behavior even more powerfully than policies or mission statements. A motivationally healthy culture is one that rewards ethical initiative, encourages professional reflection, and promotes continuous learning and feedback. In contrast, toxic cultures—marked by punitive oversight, political favoritism, or suppression of dissent—can demoralize even the most intrinsically motivated officers.

Transparency, inclusion, and dialogue must be hallmarks of the future organizational culture. Officers should have channels to express concerns, contribute to decision-making, and receive feedback that is developmental rather than merely evaluative. Psychological safety—the belief that one can take interpersonal risks without fear of punishment or humiliation—is a strong predictor of team learning, innovation, and performance (Edmondson, 1999). When officers feel safe to voice ethical concerns, share new ideas, or admit mistakes, the agency becomes more adaptable and resilient.

Leadership must also dispel the myth that motivation is static or innate. As research in motivation theory has shown, motivation is a renewable and situational resource, influenced by factors such as task design, interpersonal climate, leadership style, and institutional support (Amabile & Kramer, 2011). Officers may enter the profession with high levels of achievement motivation, but whether that drive is sustained depends largely on the culture they enter and the leaders who shape it. Ongoing mentorship, recognition, and access to developmental opportunities are essential tools for maintaining long-term motivational health.

Finally, the future of motivational leadership in policing must embrace adaptive leadership—a model that emphasizes the capacity to navigate complexity, listen actively, and respond flexibly to the changing needs of individuals and communities (Heifetz, Grashow,

& Linsky, 2009). In a world of dynamic public expectations, evolving social norms, and rapidly shifting operational demands, rigid hierarchical models are increasingly insufficient. Instead, leaders must be facilitators of purpose, guiding officers to reconnect with the deeper meaning of their work while modeling humility, learning, and psychological presence.

In conclusion, motivational leadership is not a soft skill—it is a strategic necessity for the future of ethical, effective, and sustainable policing. Agencies that invest in cultivating leaders who understand the psychological dimensions of motivation will be better equipped to retain talent, respond to crises, and build public trust in a volatile and interconnected world.

Future Research Directions

The integration of motivational theory into policing offers a rich and underexplored frontier for empirical inquiry. Despite significant advancements in organizational psychology and motivation science, the application of these frameworks in law enforcement remains sporadic and uneven. As policing institutions face increasing demands for transparency, accountability, and community trust, there is a growing imperative to generate evidence-based insights on how motivation operates—and how it can be effectively cultivated—within the complex and high-stakes environment of policing.

One essential direction for future research involves longitudinal studies that examine how motivational orientations—such as achievement (nAch), affiliation (nAff), and power (nPow), as conceptualized by McClelland (1961)—evolve over the course of an officer's career. Such studies can investigate how motivation is influenced by key turning points, including academy training, field assignments, traumatic incidents, promotions, and administrative reforms. Tracking these variables over time can illuminate how intrinsic motivation may be sustained, suppressed, or reactivated in response to shifting personal and organizational dynamics (Van Gelderen et al., 2011). This longitudinal approach is critical for designing interventions that not only spark motivation at recruitment but sustain it across decades of service.

A second promising avenue lies in comparative and cross-cultural research. As policing becomes increasingly interconnected across borders—through joint operations, international aid programs, and global knowledge exchanges—it becomes vital to understand how cultural values shape motivational expression. Building on Hofstede's (2001) dimensions of culture and the GLOBE study (House et al., 2004), researchers can examine how constructs like autonomy, hierarchy, collectivism, and uncertainty avoidance influence what motivates officers in different regions. These studies would have immediate implications for multinational police cooperation, peacekeeping missions, and training exchanges that aim to foster common ethical and performance standards while respecting cultural context.

Moreover, there is a need for experimental and quasi-experimental studies that evaluate the effectiveness of specific motivational interventions within policing environments. For example, controlled trials could assess the impact of values-affirmation exercises—brief writing tasks that reinforce core personal values—on officer resilience and ethical decision-making (Sherman et al., 2009). Other studies might test the effects of structured mentorship programs on retention and career satisfaction, or compare the outcomes of different feedback models (e.g., evaluative vs. developmental) on trainee performance and growth mindset. Such research would provide law enforcement agencies with practical tools supported by causal evidence, rather than anecdote or tradition.

An especially important and timely area for inquiry concerns the intersection of motivation with the experiences of individuals from diverse populations. Officers from varying demographic backgrounds—whether by race, gender, cultural identity, or professional rank—may follow different motivational paths depending on their sense of belonging, perceived fairness, and access to meaningful opportunity within the organization (Morin, 2020). Future research should examine how motivational climate varies across different segments of the workforce and how developmental strategies, such as mentorship or training, can be customized to support engagement and performance across this spectrum. For example, do mentorship programs yield better outcomes when mentors and mentees share similar life experiences? Do institutional messages about purpose and responsibility resonate differently depending on cultural or personal context? Investigating these questions is essential for building systems that recognize and maximize the motivational strengths of a broadly representative police force.

Additionally, future studies could explore how technological change interacts with motivation. As artificial intelligence, predictive analytics, and body-worn cameras become more prevalent, how do these tools affect officers' sense of autonomy, purpose, or perceived control? Do data-driven environments enhance or erode intrinsic motivation, particularly if officers feel surveilled or reduced to metrics? Understanding these dynamics will be critical for designing future systems that support rather than suppress motivational health in technologically advanced agencies.

Finally, motivational science should be integrated into policy research, examining how the design and communication of policies influence behavior not through coercion, but through motivational alignment. This includes performance evaluation systems, use-of-force policies, wellness programs, and promotion criteria. By measuring how these structures interact with motivational drives—through both qualitative and quantitative methods—researchers can help agencies craft policies that do not merely demand compliance but inspire commitment.

In sum, the future of motivation research in policing must be multidimensional, interdisciplinary, and inclusive, drawing from psychology, criminology, organizational behavior, and cultural studies. As policing itself continues to evolve, the research agenda must evolve with it—ensuring that motivation is not just studied as an individual trait but understood as a dynamic, context-sensitive force that shapes and is shaped by the institutions and cultures in which officers serve.

Closing Reflections: Driven to Serve

The future of policing will not be defined solely by body-worn cameras, predictive analytics, or revised use-of-force protocols. While these tools and reforms are undoubtedly important, they are insufficient if not matched by a parallel investment in the inner architecture of officer motivation. At its core, policing remains a profoundly human endeavor—one that relies on discretion, moral reasoning, empathy, and judgment in complex, unpredictable environments. Thus, the true fulcrum of reform and progress lies not just in technology or structure, but in the quality and motivation of those who serve.

Officers who are intrinsically driven—by a sense of purpose, a desire for mastery, and a commitment to justice—represent the most resilient and ethical assets in any department. These individuals do not merely follow rules or comply with protocols; they internalize the mission of public service and act from a place of personal alignment with institutional values (Ryan & Deci, 2000; McClelland, 1961). They are the officers who show up for community events after their shift ends, who reflect on their decisions in quiet moments, who mentor younger colleagues not because they have to, but because they believe in building something greater than themselves. This form of motivation—deep, enduring, and self-regulated—is what separates a compliant workforce from a committed one.

Yet such motivation does not emerge spontaneously. It is cultivated—or conversely, eroded—by the systems, cultures, and leadership structures that surround it. Agencies that prioritize output over integrity, or discipline over development, may suppress the very motivation they hope to inspire. Conversely, institutions that nurture motivational health through inclusive leadership, meaningful work, transparent communication, and continuous growth can unlock higher levels of performance, satisfaction, and ethical conduct across the board (Maslach & Leiter, 2016; Brown & Treviño, 2006).

To "serve because one is driven" requires a transformation in how we think about human potential. It calls on departments to view officers not just as agents of law, but as stewards of public trust—professionals whose internal motivations must be protected, shaped, and aligned with the evolving needs of society. This means embedding motivational principles into recruitment, training, supervision, policy design, and wellness programming. It means valuing not only what officers do, but why they do it.

As this book has argued, the science of motivation is not merely academic—it is actionable. Tools such as motivational assessments, scenario-based training, mentorship models, and inclusive leadership practices can be deployed to build cultures where purpose and performance reinforce one another. These are not soft ideals, but hard imperatives. In a world marked by rising complexity, public scrutiny, and moral ambiguity, agencies that fail to cultivate intrinsic motivation may find themselves with a technically capable but spiritually disengaged workforce—precisely the kind of force most vulnerable to burnout, misconduct, and attrition.

Conversely, law enforcement organizations that institutionalize motivational development stand to gain a durable competitive advantage. They will be better equipped to attract the right candidates, retain high-performing staff, manage change, and earn the trust of the communities they serve. More importantly, they will become environments where officers can thrive—not just survive—through careers that are professionally rewarding and personally meaningful.

In closing, the vision of policing we must advance is not one where officers act simply because they are commanded to, but because they are compelled by purpose, fortified by support, and sustained by a culture that sees their motivation as a vital asset. This is the foundation of legitimacy, the anchor of reform, and the heart of what it means to be driven to serve.

References

Amabile, T. M., Hill, K. G., Hennessey, B. A., & Tighe, E. M. (1994). The Work Preference Inventory: Assessing intrinsic and extrinsic motivational orientations. *Journal of Personality and Social Psychology*, 66(5), 950.

Ames, C. (1992). Classrooms: Goals, structures, and student motivation. *Journal of Educational Psychology*, 84(3), 261–271.

Bandura, A. (1997). *Self-efficacy: The exercise of control*. New York: W.H. Freeman.

Barbuto, J. E., & Scholl, R. W. (1998). Motivation sources inventory: Development and validation of new scales to measure an integrative taxonomy of motivation. *Psychological Reports*, 82(3_suppl), 1011–1022.

Bass, B. M., & Riggio, R. E. (2006). Transformational leadership (2nd ed.). Mahwah, NJ: Lawrence Erlbaum Associates.

Bayley, D. H. (1991). *Forces of Order: Policing Modern Japan.* University of California Press.

Brown, M. E., & Treviño, L. K. (2006). Ethical leadership: A review and future directions. *The Leadership Quarterly*, 17(6), 595-616.

Brough, P., & Frame, R. (2004). Predicting police job satisfaction and turnover intentions: The role of social support and police organizational variables. *New Zealand Journal of Psychology*, 33(1), 8–16.

Chappell, A. T. (2007). Community policing: Training, definitions, and policy implications. *Policing: An International Journal of Police Strategies & Management, 30*(4), 535–547.

College of Policing. (2019). *The National Policing Curriculum.* Retrieved from https://www.college.police.uk

Conti, N., & Nolan, J. J. (2005). Policing the platonic cave: Ethics and efficacy in police training. *Policing and Society, 15*(2), 166–186.

Cooper, C. L., Davidson, M., & Robinson, P. (1982). Stress in the police service. *Journal of Occupational Medicine*, 24(1), 30–6.

Deci, E. L., & Ryan, R. M. (1985). *Intrinsic motivation and self-determination in human behavior*. Springer.

Deci, E. L., & Ryan, R. M. (2000). The "what" and "why" of goal pursuits: Human needs and the self-determination of behavior. *Psychological Inquiry, 11*(4), 227–268. https://doi.org/10.1207/S15327965PLI1104_01

Densten, I. L. (2002). Clarifying inspirational motivation and its relationship to extra effort. *Leadership & Organization Development Journal, 23*(1), 40–44. https://doi.org/10.1108/01437730210414510

Den Hartog, D. N., House, R. J., Hanges, P. J., Ruiz-Quintanilla, S. A., & Dorfman, P. W. (1999). Culture specific and cross-culturally generalizable implicit leadership theories: Are attributes of charismatic/transformational leadership universally endorsed? *The Leadership Quarterly, 10*(2), 219–256.

Edmondson, A. (1999). Psychological safety and learning behavior in work teams. *Administrative Science Quarterly*, 44(2), 350–383.

Gagné, M., & Deci, E. L. (2005). Self-determination theory and work motivation. Journal of Organizational Behavior, 26(4), 331–362. https://doi.org/10.1002/job.322

Goleman, D. (2006). *Emotional Intelligence: Why It Can Matter More Than IQ*. Bantam.

Kolb, D. A. (1984). *Experiential learning: Experience as the source of learning and development.* Englewood Cliffs, NJ: Prentice-Hall.

Hackman, J. R., & Oldham, G. R. (1976). Motivation through the design of work: Test of a theory. Organizational Behavior and Human Performance, 16(2), 250–279. https://doi.org/10.1016/0030-5073(76)90016-7

Hersey, P., Blanchard, K. H., & Johnson, D. E. (2012). Management of organizational behavior: Leading human resources (10th ed.). Upper Saddle River, NJ: Pearson.

Herzberg, F. (1966). *Work and the nature of man.* Cleveland: World Publishing Company.

Hofstede, G. (2001). *Culture's Consequences: Comparing Values, Behaviors, Institutions and Organizations Across Nations.* Sage Publications.

Ingram, J. R., Paoline, E. A., & Terrill, W. (2013). A multilevel framework for understanding police culture: The role of the workgroup. *Criminology*, 51(2), 365–397.

Johnson, R. R. (2012). *Police Officer Job Satisfaction: A Multidimensional Analysis*. LFB Scholarly Publishing.

Johnson, R. R., & Button, D. M. (2000). Motivation in police work: A study of basic recruit training. *Police Quarterly*, 3(1), 5–24.

Kaptein, M. (2011). Understanding unethical behavior by unraveling ethical culture. *Human Relations, 64*(6), 843–869. https://doi.org/10.1177/0018726710385252

Kellerman, B. (2004). *Bad leadership: What it is, how it happens, why it matters*. Harvard Business Review Press.

Kernis, M. H., & Goldman, B. M. (2006). A multicomponent conceptualization of authenticity: Theory and research. *Advances in Experimental Social Psychology*, 38, 283-357.

Kouzes, J. M., & Posner, B. Z. (2017). The leadership challenge: How to make extraordinary things happen in organizations (6th ed.). Hoboken, NJ: Jossey-Bass.

Litz, B. T., Stein, N., Delaney, E., Lebowitz, L., Nash, W. P., Silva, C., & Maguen, S. (2009). Moral injury and moral repair in war veterans: A preliminary model and intervention strategy. *Clinical Psychology Review, 29*(8), 695-706.

Lipman-Blumen, J. (2005). *The allure of toxic leaders: Why we follow destructive bosses and corrupt politicians—and how we can survive them*. Oxford University Press.

London, M., & Smither, J. W. (2002). Feedback orientation, feedback culture, and the longitudinal performance management process. *Human Resource Management Review*, 12(1), 81–100.

Maslach, C., & Leiter, M. P. (2016). *Burnout: A multidimensional perspective*. In

Cooper, C. L. (Ed.), *Theories of Organizational Stress* (pp. 68-85). Oxford University Press.

Mastrofski, S. D., Ritti, R. R., & Hoffmaster, D. (2007). Making sense of community policing: A theory-based analysis. *Police Quarterly, 10*(3), 344–365.

McAdams, D. P. (2001). The psychology of life stories. *Review of General Psychology, 5*(2), 100–122.

McClelland, D. C. (1961). *The Achieving Society.* Princeton: Van Nostrand.

McClelland, D. C., & Burnham, D. H. (1976). Power is the great motivator. Harvard Business Review, 54(2), 100–110.

Maslow, A. H. (1943). A theory of human motivation. Psychological Review, 50(4), 370–396.

Miller, L. (2006). Practical police psychology: Stress management and crisis intervention for law enforcement. *Charles C. Thomas Publisher*.

Papazoglou, K., & Andersen, J. P. (2014). A guide to enhancing police resilience: The integration of wellness and psychological training in police academies. *International Journal of Emergency Mental Health and Human Resilience, 16*(1), 356-362.

Perry, J. L., & Wise, L. R. (1990). The motivational bases of public service. Public Administration Review, 50(3), 367–373.

Pink, D. H. (2009). Drive: The surprising truth about what motivates us. New York, NY: Riverhead Books.

Punch, M. (2009). *Police corruption: Deviance, accountability and reform in policing*. Routledge.

Rest, J. R., & Narvaez, D. (Eds.). (1994). *Moral development in the professions: Psychology and applied ethics*. Lawrence Erlbaum Associates.

Ryan, R. M., & Deci, E. L. (2000). Self-determination theory and the facilitation of intrinsic motivation, social development, and well-being. *American Psychologist, 55*(1), 68–78.

Reiner, R. (2010). *The Politics of the Police* (4th ed.). Oxford University Press.

Schuler, H., & Prochaska, M. (2001). *The Achievement Motivation Inventory* (AMI). Manual. Göttingen: Hogrefe.

Schein, E. H. (2010). *Organizational Culture and Leadership* (4th ed.). Jossey-Bass.

Skolnick, J. H., & Fyfe, J. J. (1993). *Above the law: Police and the excessive use of force*. Free Press.

Skolnick, J. H. (2002). Corruption and the blue code of silence. *Police Practice and Research, 3*(1), 7–19. https://doi.org/10.1080/713803841

Skogan, W. G. (2006). *Police and Community in Chicago: A Tale of Three Cities*. Oxford

Socorro, R. (2012). Achievement Motivation of Police Officers in a Florida Urban Setting. (Doctoral dissertation). Barry University.

Schaible, L. M., & Six, M. (2016). Emotional strategies of police officers: Control, venting, and minimization. *Justice Quarterly*, 33(2), 333–355.

Treviño, L. K., & Brown, M. E. (2004). Managing to be ethical: Debunking five business ethics myths. *Academy of Management Perspectives*, 18(2), 69–81.

Tummers, L. G., & Knies, E. (2013). Leadership and meaningful work in the public sector. *Public Administration Review*, 73(6), 859–868.

UNODC. (2021). *Police Reform in Colombia: Lessons from Transitional Contexts.* United Nations Office on Drugs and Crime.

Van Gelderen, B. R., Bakker, A. B., Konijn, E. A., & Demerouti, E. (2011). Daily suppression of discrete emotions during the work of police service workers and criminal investigation officers. *Anxiety, Stress, & Coping*, 24(5), 515-537.

Violanti, J. M., Charles, L. E., McCanlies, E., Hartley, T. A., Baughman, P., Andrew, M. E., & Burchfiel, C. M. (2017). Police stressors and health: A state-of-the-art review. *Policing: An International Journal*, 40(4), 642–656.

Waddington, P. A. J., & Wright, M. A. (2008). Professionalism and paramilitarism in the British police. *British Journal of Criminology, 48*(5), 600–619.

Winter, D. G. (1991). *Motivation and Personality: Handbook of Thematic Content Analysis*. Cambridge University Press.

Vroom, V. H. (1964). *Work and Motivation*. New York: Wiley.

Zhao, J., He, N., & Lovrich, N. P. (2002). Predicting the job satisfaction of police officers: Work environment versus demographic predictors. *Justice Quarterly*, 19(1), 53–85.

Yukl, G. (2013). Leadership in organizations (8th ed.). Boston, MA: Pearson Education.

Zimmerman, B. J. (2000). Self-efficacy: An essential motive to learn. *Contemporary Educational Psychology, 25*(1), 82–91.

www.ingramcontent.com/pod-product-compliance
Ingram Content Group UK Ltd.
Pitfield, Milton Keynes, MK11 3LW, UK
UKHW022031041026
15591UKWH00012B/612

9 798330 248964